Margo Wardlow

CATE

**HOPI CHIEF**
(Drawn by Howard McCormick)

AMERICAN MUSEUM OF NATURAL HISTORY

# INDIANS
# OF THE SOUTHWEST

By PLINY EARLE GODDARD

LATE CURATOR OF ETHNOLOGY

HANDBOOK SERIES No. 2

(FOURTH EDITION)

NEW YORK

1931

❈ AMERICAN · MUSEUM · PRESS ❈

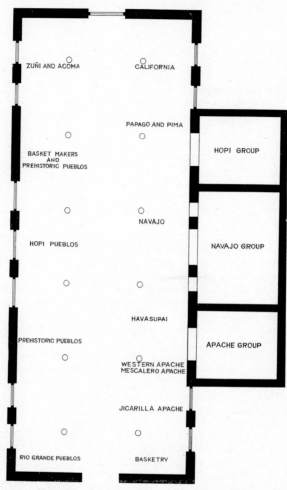

HALL FOR THE INDIANS OF THE SOUTHWEST

Southwestern cultures, prehistoric and historic, are presented in one exhibition hall, in which is also temporarily displayed an ethnological collection, including the basketry, of the California Area. The exhibits in the hall, therefore, are comprised in four main divisions: the prehistoric peoples, the present day Pueblo, the nomadic tribes, and the Californians.

Except for the special exhibition of basketry in one alcove, the exhibits are arranged according to tribal groups: the Jicarilla, Mescalero,

San Carlos, and White Mountain Apache, the Havasupai, the Navajo, and the Papago and Pima being shown in the order named. The modern Pueblo, except for the villages on the Rio Grande in New Mexico are also presented tribally, the Hopi villages and Zuni being treated in detail. The remainder of the hall is given over to a presentation of the cultural remains of the prehistoric inhabitants of the area, the collections shown, like those for the living peoples, resulting almost entirely from the work of Museum expeditions.

Archaeologically, the area is also well represented. Here the unit of exhibition is geographical or restricted to particular ruin sites, viz., the Galisteo Basin, the Gila River District, the Mimbres Valley, Pueblo Bonito, Grand Gulch, the Mesa Verde, the Little Colorado District, the Aztec Ruin, Canyons del Muerto and de Chelly. However, a beginning has been made in the demonstration of Southwestern chronology through such presentations as the tree ring method of dating ruins, and the sequences of pottery on the Galisteo Valley and of Basket Maker III pottery in the San Juan Area, etc.

To clarify and elucidate these ethnological and archaeological exhibits further there have been added miniature models of Pueblo villages, modern and prehistoric, models of cliff ruins, and three life size groups in alcoves at one side of the hall depicting the home or ceremonial life of the Apache, Navajo, and Hopi, respectively.

The collections in this hall have been obtained chiefly by Museum expeditions and donations. The Hyde Expedition resulted in a great number of archaeological specimens, many of which are still in storage. From 1909 to 1921 there were obtained by funds provided by Archer M. Huntington for the study of the primitive peoples of the Southwest, the ethnological collections from the Rio Grande and Hopi pueblos and from the Apache, Pima, and Papago tribes; and the archaeological specimens from Aztec, the Galisteo historic and prehistoric ruins, and from Old Cochiti. The investigations of the chronologically important sites in Canyon del Muerto and Canyon de Chelly, resulting in collections from the Basket Maker periods were made possible by the generosity of the late Ogden Mills. A large number of the baskets were donated by Dr. James Douglas; the Navajo blankets represent the generosity of Mrs. Russell Sage and the late J. Pierpont Morgan.

The California collections were acquired by the Huntington Expedition, conducted by Dr. Roland B. Dixon; by the purchase of the Briggs collection of baskets through the generosity of George Foster Peabody; by the work of Miss Constance Goddard DuBois in southern California; and through exchanges.

# PREFACE TO THE FOURTH EDITION

The author of this book died before the previous edition was exhausted; consequently, the necessary revisions to bring the text abreast of advancing knowledge have been made by the Editor. Originally, this book was designed as a comprehensive guide to the collections in the Museum, but was intended at the same time to offer a review of the facts concerning both the historic and the prehistoric aboriginal inhabitants of that well known part of the United States, properly spoken of as the Southwest. To quote from the original preface by the author:—

"Although a great deal of time has been devoted to the study of the native peoples of the Southwest and the prehistoric ruins in that region by many ethnologists and archaeologists our knowledge of them is still far from complete. There are many ruins which have never been visited by a trained observer; the Rio Grande peoples persistently oppose the study of their ceremonial life; and notwithstanding the great number of treatises on the Hopi, there is none of them which gives a satisfactory account of their everyday life and of their social customs and organization.

The author has first-hand knowledge of the Athapascan-speaking peoples only. The accounts given in the following pages of the prehistoric and sedentary peoples have been drawn from published papers by many authors. The most important works on the Southwest are listed at the end of this book and in them will be found the sources of the information here given."

The reader desiring a more comprehensive statement of the prehistoric Southwest is referred to Doctor A. V. Kidder's *Southwestern Archaeology*.

# CONTENTS

## CHAPTER V

## MAPS AND ILLUSTRATIONS

# INTRODUCTION

The region which is called the Southwest in the title of this book is a natural geographical division lying south of the higher and more definite ranges of the Rocky Mountains. It is drained by the upper portion of the Rio Grande and its tributary, the Pecos, and by the Colorado River and its three main eastern branches, the San Juan, the Little Colorado, and the Gila. There are considerable ranges of mountains between the Rio Grande and the Pecos, and mountain masses north of the San Juan and at the head of the Gila. Somewhat isolated mountain peaks, such as the San Francisco Peaks (12,794) and San Mateo (11,389), rise here and there. The Continental Divide, however, is for the most part unmarked by any definite elevation.

The northern portion of the region is a high plateau with an average elevation of about 6,000 feet. This plateau is so sculptured that, generally speaking, the walls of both the elevations and the depressions are vertical. Instead of rounded hills and V-shaped valleys, we have, for the most part, flat-topped mesas and sheer-walled canyons. South and west of the watershed, between the Little Colorado and the Salt, the country decreases in elevation very abruptly and then slopes to the low lying desert at the mouth of the Gila.

Over much of the region evidences of considerable volcanic activity are found, consisting of extensive lava fields, dikes of projecting lava which can be followed for many miles, numerous extinct craters, and active hot springs.

The rainfall varies considerably according to the elevation, but is greater than is generally supposed. At

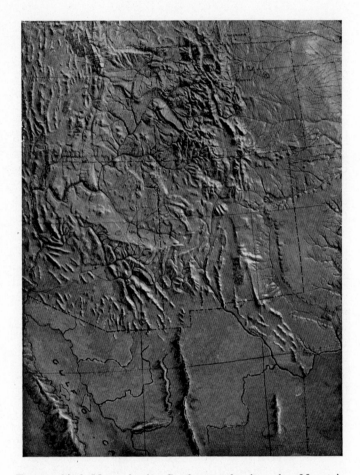

Topographical Map of the Southwest, showing the Mountain
Ranges and an Elevated Plateau in the Middle

Flagstaff it is 24 inches and over the greater portion of the region as much as 10 or 15 inches. Along the lower Gila, however, it is as low as 1 or 2 inches, resulting in a veritable desert.

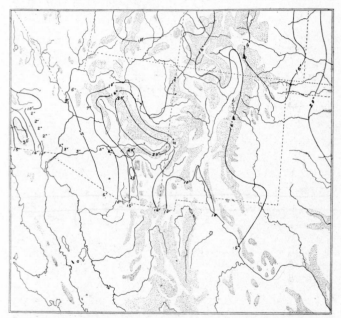

Distribution of Forests and Rainfall. Shaded Portion indicates Timber and the Black Lines Rainfall Areas

The vegetation varies with the altitude and the rainfall. On the higher mountains and the more elevated plateaus are great forests of yellow pine with occasional Douglas spruce. The middle elevations are clothed with smaller trees, such as piñon, a dwarf pine, cedar, juniper, and cypress. Small-growing oaks and mesquite bushes are also characteristic of the lesser

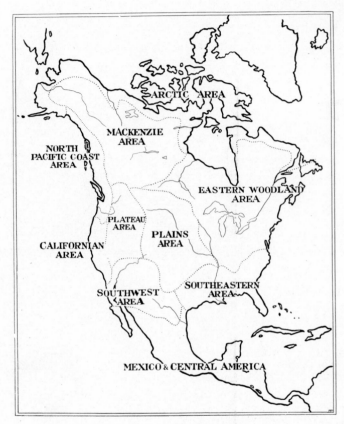

Culture Areas in North America

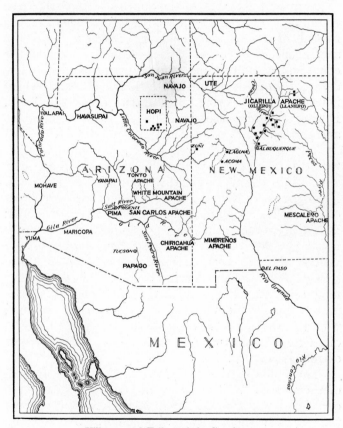

Villages and Tribes of the Southwest

elevations. The river banks are usually lined with cottonwoods and sycamores, giving the general appearance of vegetation.

More characteristic of the Southwest than the trees enumerated above, are the century plant or agave, the mescal of the Spanish-speaking residents, and the several species of yucca. The more arid portions of the country, the unwatered upper district and the low desert regions have many varieties of cacti which flourish through droughts and the occasional rains. During the rainy season in August, flowers are abundant and general verdure is common.

The aridity of the region is more impressive in regard to the atmosphere itself. The snows of winter vanish into the air leaving little surface water or mud. During most of the year the dryness of the air enables one to see for a long distance and observe small details; in other words, atmospheric perspective is largely wanting. This is at first very bewildering to the visitor who has been accustomed to judge distance by the amount of intervening haze. While the distant mountains are not obscured, the atmosphere does impart to them shades of blue and purple which, combined with the varying local color of the landscape and the often gorgeous dawns and sunsets, make the Southwest extremely colorful.

The fauna of the Southwest is that characteristic of the western United States in general. There were occasional visitors from Mexico, such as the macaw, the peccary, and possibly the jaguar. Of economic importance were the turkey, quail, deer, antelope, rabbits, and wood-rats. Elk occupied the region but were not easily killed. The bison, on the other hand, were only available when hunting trips were undertaken to the region east of the Pecos, which, according to an old saying, the buffalo did not cross.

The natives occupying the Southwest are representatives of the race known as American Indian. Their common characteristics are: a warm chocolate color, straight black hair, brown eyes, wide faces, and high cheek bones. In other respects the Southwestern peoples exhibit considerable variety. The accompanying table shows the Maricopa, averaging 68.8 inches in height on the one hand, and the Pueblo peoples on the Rio Grande averaging a little more than 64 inches.

|  | Inches |  | Inches |
|---|---|---|---|
| Maricopa | 68.8 | Walapai | 66.3 |
| Yuma | 67.7 | Isleta | 662. |
| Pima | 67.6 | Mescalero Apache | 65.9 |
| Mohave | 67.5 | Southern Ute | 65.6 |
| Jicarilla Apache | 67.4 | San Juan | 65.3 |
| Navajo | 67.4 | Acoma | 64.9 |
| White River Apache | 67.3 | Taos | 64.6 |
| Papago | 67.2 | Hopi | 64.4 |
| Havasupai | 67.1 | Zuñi | 64.3 |
| Yavapai | 67.08 | Jemez | 64.05 |
| San Carlos Apache | 66.7 | Sia | 63.9 |

The cephalic index, or proportion of the length to the breadth of the head, has been much used in racial description and classification. The skulls recovered from the Basket Maker burials of southern Utah are extremely long and narrow. Of the modern peoples of the Southwest only the Pima and Papago and some of the people of Taos are long-headed. The heads of the remainder of the prehistoric people; those of the present-day Maricopa, Yuma, Mohave; and most of the sedentary people, the Hopi, the Zuñi, and the Rio

Grande Pueblos generally, are moderately broad. Only the Apache, the Havasupai, and the Walapai have heads which are exceedingly broad as compared with their lengths.

It is apparent then that the inhabitants of the Southwest are of two, perhaps three, physical types which have either migrated to that region from different places and at different times, or which, after long residence in the Southwest, have resulted from the breaking up of a previously uniform type. These types, having become established by either of the methods mentioned above, have remained distinct in consequence of a cultural, social, and political grouping which has prevented extended intermarriage.

The languages spoken in the Southwest present similar variations and lead to analogous conclusions. Two of the larger linguistic stocks of North America, the Athapascan and Shoshonean, are represented in the region.

The Navajo and the various Apache tribes, constituting fifty-eight per cent of the population, are Athapascan speaking. Their dialects do not differ greatly from each other, and have certain characteristics in common which are not found elsewhere. Related languages are spoken in Alaska and over much of western Canada and along the Pacific coast in Oregon and northern California.

The Hopi, in culture a typical Pueblo people, speak a Shoshonean language, linking them to the Ute and related tribes who occupy the Great Basin to the north. The Pima and Papago are closely connected linguistically with the inhabitants of the Mexican Sierra. The tribes inhabiting western Arizona are chiefly Yuman in speech, related in that respect to certain tribes in southern California and near the Gulf of California. On the other hand, there are three linguistic stocks in the Southwest which have no known connections elsewhere. These are the Zuñi language, spoken at the pueblo of that name and its outlying villages; the Keresan dialects, spoken at Acoma and certain villages in the Rio Grande drainage; and the Tewan languages, spoken along the Rio Grande and at one of the Hopi villages.

The existence of a remote but definite linguistic relationship has been established between the Shoshonean languages represented in the Southwest by the Ute and the Hopi, and the Piman languages, which include Pima, Papago, and the dialects of northwestern Mexico. Included in this larger group, known as the Uto-Aztecan, is Nahua, the language of the ancient Mexicans or Aztec.

The obvious conclusions from these linguistic facts are that peoples speaking different languages have invaded the Southwest at various times. The assumption is that people of Uto-Aztecan speech occupied the Great Basin, the western part of Arizona, and the Sierra of Mexico in early times. Free communication between the Hopi and the Ute of the north, and the Pima and other tribes of the south must have ceased many generations ago, either because the territory between them was unoccupied or because its inhabitants were alien in speech. The considerable difference between the Piman and the Shoshonean languages under average circumstances would only result after many centuries of separation. It is also proper to assume that the Pueblo peoples mentioned above as speaking distinct languages, the Zuñi, the Keres, and the Tewa, have been in the Southwest for a very long time. The Athapascan-speaking Navajo and Apache are by no means recent comers if one judges in terms of history and of the European occupation of America. The evidence indicates that all the Athapascan-speaking tribes of the Southwest once formed a single community and developed a common language. Since that time a wider distribution or impeded intercourse has resulted in this once common language being broken into fairly distinct dialects. This appears to have taken place prior to the Spanish period which began in 1539.

When our knowledge of their physical characteristics has been increased and made available by publication it may be possible to collate it with linguistic and cultural conclusions and determine the early movements and amalgamations of the Southwestern peoples.

So far we have dealt with data secured by observation upon living Indians, as given in historical documents, and recorded by anthropologists, but every visitor to the Southwest knows that remains of prehistoric cultures are abundant, some of which appear to possess a respectable antiquity. Great progress has been made by archaeologists specializing in this field, especially in the drainage of the San Juan River and the upper Rio Grande. It is now certain not only that the Pueblo tribes first seen by the Spanish explorers were of ancient origin, but were preceded by non-Pueblo cultures. Before 1910 little was known as to the relative ages of these prehistoric remains, but the detailed studies of pottery initiated by the archaeologists, N. C. Nelson of this Museum and A. V. Kidder of Phillips Academy, Andover, Massachusetts, soon developed a method by which stratification of pottery types could be used as a key to rank in age. Following this lead Earl H. Morris of this Museum, S. J. Guernsey of the Peabody Museum, Harvard University, and others have brought together such a wealth of data that we now possess a reliable outline of the prehistory of the whole San Juan area and its immediate margins, the probability being that this outline will be generally applicable to the whole of the Southwest and much of the adjoining territory.

Further, it is becoming clearer that the drainage of the San Juan and its fringes was the center of development for the successive prehistoric cultures of the Southwest. Two main types of prehistoric culture are distinguished, the so-called Basket Makers and the Pueblo Dwellers. Each of these types passed through a number of stages, the characteristics of which are now so well known that all the many hundreds of ruins and sites observed can be assigned to their proper periods. We thus come to realize that the Southwest the Spanish explorers found in 1539 was of ancient origin, the forgotten history of which was destined to be recovered by American scholars of the twentieth century.

# CHAPTER I

## THE ANCIENT PEOPLES

The information here presented concerning the culture of the primitive peoples of the Southwest falls into two classes. Knowledge of a people obtained by direct observation and by intercourse with them is called ethnological, while that which is secured from a study of their houses and manufactures left after they have disappeared is called archaeological. There are large regions in the Southwest where there are plentiful ruins which have been unoccupied since the first arrival of Europeans in 1539. Whatever we know concerning the culture of these ancient peoples must be either directly observed or inferred from the relation which these ruins and other remains bear to each other and to similar structures and objects still used by living peoples.

Much has been lost beyond any possibility of reconstruction. We know nothing of the language spoken by these peoples; their social customs can only be surmised in certain minor particulars; and their religion is only to be inferred from objects that must have had a ceremonial use. While much has been lost, our knowledge is constantly increasing through the systematic examination of the ruins and their contents.

Because large regions have been unoccupied for centuries we need not assume the inhabitants perished. It is more probable they moved to other localities where their descendants were found by the Spaniards. Whence or when came the ancient peoples we do not know. They may have been in this region for several thousands of years. We do know that after they came they passed through an interesting development.

## DISTRIBUTION

As a logical beginning of this chapter, a review of the geographical distribution of ruins and archaeological materials seems necessary.

As might be expected in a semi-arid region, the agricultural population in prehistoric times was concentrated at the higher elevations where the rainfall was greatest and in the river valleys where irrigation could be practised easily.

*San Juan.* One of the most important regions anciently occupied was that watered by the northern tributaries of the San Juan River. These streams are fed by the snows of the mountains of southern Colorado and Utah. At some distance from their sources they are confined in sheer-walled canyons which unite with each other as they approach the San Juan, which enters the Colorado above the Grand Canyon. Some of the ruins are on the table-lands between the streams, others are at the heads of the canyons, and many are in the canyons themselves either on their floors or under their overhanging walls. Cliff Palace and Spruce Tree House in the Mesa Verde National Park are two of the largest and best known ruins standing under cliffs. In the valley of the Animas, opposite the town of Aztec, is a very large ruin near the river.

Among the southern tributaries is Chaco Canyon. Here is a cluster of eleven large ruins which evidently represent an important political group of prehistoric villages. One of these, Pueblo Bonito, is hardly surpassed in size and interest anywhere. Canyon del Muerto and Canyon de Chelly, which join Chinlee Valley, have many ruins for the most part on ledges under overhanging walls.

Archaeologically this is at present the most important area, because it has been the most intensively studied. It is believed by many to contribute the most important culture area of the whole Southwest.

*Rio Grande.* On the western side of the Rio Grande Valley are many large ruins. Some of them are in the valley of the Rio Chama; many are on the mesas of the Pajarito Plateau to the south; and others in the canyon of the Rito de los Frijoles. In the valley of the Rio Grande itself and along its eastern tributaries, are ruins antedating the Spanish era, others which were deserted prior to and during the Pueblo rebellion, 1680–1682, and a number of villages which have persisted until the present day.

*Pecos.* The pueblo of Pecos on the river of that name was occupied until 1838. In prehistoric times there were many pueblos for forty miles along the valley. Between the Rio Pecos and the Rio Grande are many ruins and evidences of former occupation by a sedentary, pottery-making people. Some of these ruins, notably Abo, Quarai, and Tabira or Gran Quivira, were still occupied under Spanish rule.

*Gila.* Along the upper tributaries of the Gila and Salt rivers there are evidences of a fairly dense population which occupied cliff-dwellings and community houses standing in the valleys. These were built of stone. Farther down these rivers, the houses were built mostly with earthen walls; only mounds of earth and boulders now mark the outlines of the walls. Not far from Florence, Arizona, near the Gila River, is the large ruin called Casa Grande, a number of houses surrounded by a defensive wall. These are of solid adobe construction and resemble ruins in Chihuahua, Mexico, known as Casas Grandes. The Rio Verde which flows into the Salt from the north has a great number and a great variety of ruins in its valley which seems to mark the western limit of this prehistoric culture.

*Little Colorado.* There remains another large tributary of the Colorado which flows through the heart of the Southwest, the Little Colorado. Within its drainage are many prehistoric ruins, villages with old Spanish churches, now deserted, and the still inhabited villages of the Hopi and Zuñi.

## THE SUCCESSIVE CULTURE PERIODS

We are again reminded that what we know of the Southwest preceding 1539 is the result of archaeological research. The American occupation of the new territory acquired after the war with Mexico soon brought to notice its prehistoric treasures, ushering in an era of archaeological exploration in which such leaders as Bandelier, Fewkes, Holmes, Hough, Jackson, Mindeleff, Nordenskiöld, and Prudden were conspicuous. By the first decade of the twentieth century, a general survey of the area had been accomplished and a wealth of museum material collected. Following this inventory of sites and materials came a period of study directed toward the arrangement of these data in a time sequence. Such progress has been made to date that a chronological chart has been devised reconstructing the culture history of the San Juan area as a working scheme for the whole Southwest. At a conference of specialists in this field held at Pecos, New Mexico, in 1927, a table similar to the one given here was approved, and is now generally accepted as the working basis for future research. Naturally, new data may lead to some revision of this table, but it has so far stood the test in further exploration. The terms used in this new chart differ slightly from those previously employed. First it will be noted that there are two main periods, that of the Basket Makers and of the Pueblo Builders. The latter extended into historic time, which may be said to begin with the exploration of the country by the Spaniards in 1540. Each of these periods has been subdivided, as Basket Maker I, II, and III; Pueblo I to V.

Some progress has been made in dating these periods through the researches of Dr. A. E. Douglass in tree growth as shown in logs preserved in the walls of certain ruins, as in Bonito, Aztec, Betatakin, etc. This method is fully explained elsewhere. According to the determinations made by Douglass, Pueblo Bonito was begun about 919 and achieved its final form in 1130; Cliff Palace, Mesa Verde, was built in 1073; Aztec in 1133, etc. On the basis of these specific dates it has been assumed that the Pueblo Periods run as follows:—

Pueblo V     — 1700 to the present
Pueblo IV    — 1300–1700
Pueblo III   —  900–1300
Pueblo II    — Probably 400 years
Pueblo I     — Probably 500 years

It will be noted that the tree ring data go back to 900 A.D., thus covering the Great Period, or Pueblo III only, leaving Pueblo I and II to conjecture. For these two periods the above conservative guesses have been made. Accepting these as reasonable, we see that the Basket Maker cultures seem to belong to pre-Christian time and to have their beginnings in a respectable antiquity.

## Culture Periods

*Basket Maker I*

Of this, the earliest form of culture, we have only the slenderest evidence because the people of that time had no knowledge of agriculture, led a nomadic existence, and so left very few remains. It is probable, however, that, like their descendants, the true Basket Makers, they used spear throwers, or atlatls, instead of bows; also a curved throwing club; wore clothing of skins; and had no permanent habitations. The racial type was generally Indian, but doubtless long-headed, as was that of the next period.

### Basket Maker II, or True Basket Maker

A semi-hunting, semi-agricultural culture; a single type of maize and a squash were known; skilful weaving of baskets, sandals, bags, and twisting of cord. No permanent homes, no bows and arrows; no true pottery, but at the end of the period unfired clay vessels were used, the first step in the process.

### Basket Maker III, or Post-Basket Maker

This period was marked by distinct progress. The manufacture of true pottery began; beans were raised and several varieties of maize acquired. The bow and arrow appear for the first time. Simple dwellings, partially underground, lined with stone slabs set on edge, called slab houses.

### Pueblo I, or Pre-Pueblo

Rounder headed people appear, who artificially deformed their heads. Houses of more than one room whose walls show attempts at the construction of true, horizontally coursed masonry. The turkey was domesticated, cotton cultivated and woven into cloth.

### Pueblo II

Small villages composed of unit or one-clan houses, wholly above ground and with substantial masonry walls; the subterranean kiva, or ceremonial chamber, which came into regular use in this period was derived

from the underground living room of earlier times.
Corrugated and painted pottery common.

### Pueblo III

The Great Pueblo Period in which large villages were
developed, some of the ruins of which are famous:
Spruce Tree House, Cliff Palace, Bonito, Aztec, etc.
Pottery was highly specialized in local styles. The end
of this period is marked by abandonment of the larger
centers and a general decline in the arts.

### Pueblo IV

A period of readjustment following the decay of the
great centers of Pueblo III, the preceding period. To
this period belong certain early Hopi and Zuñi ruins,
Pecos, and a number of sites in the region around Santa
Fé. At its close came the initial period of contact with
European culture as represented by the Spanish régime
in Mexico.

### Pueblo V

The historic period, from the final Spanish conquest
in 1696 to the present. The existing Pueblo villages
came into existence, for the most part in Period IV.
Modification of Pueblo culture due to Spanish, and
later, American influence.

### BASKET MAKERS

This term came into use after the publication of a
paper by George H. Pepper, describing a collection
brought to this Museum from Grand Gulch, Utah.
The high development of basketry and the absence of
pottery led this author to assume that here were the
remains of a pre-Pueblo culture. As we have seen, this
was prophetic and the priority of the term has been

respected, even though it is now known that the later
Basket Makers used pottery. While specialists in the
subject classify Basket Maker sites and materials
under three periods, there seems to have been a continuous development throughout. In general, all Basket
Maker collections contain much in common: long,
narrow, undeformed skulls; the atlatls or spear throwers; curved throwing clubs, suggesting boomerangs
but not possessing the properties that cause them to
return when thrown; excellently coiled baskets;
elaborately woven sandals, often complicated in pattern;
twined bags of unusual quality; many varieties of cord
and rope; robes of fur cloth; small fringed aprons or
skirts for women. The introduction of maize, marking
the second stage in the history of the Basket Makers,
may be considered the most important advance, since
it initiated agriculture, destined to become the economic
basis of all native Southwestern cultures. The storage
of maize began with simple cache pits in the floors of
caves and shelters. In time these became larger and
were frequently used as burial places. By the close of
the period several varieties of maize were grown,
together with squashes and beans.
      Well into the middle of Basket Maker time a semi-
subterranean pit-like house takes form, which, at the
end of Basket Maker III took the form of a circular or
oval pit, covered by a superstructure of poles, brush,
and earth. These dwellings were clustered in small
camps or villages, relatively permanent in location.
      In some respects the most interesting materials
collected from Basket Maker sites are their first attempts at pottery. These were in fact, heavy, crude,
sun-dried vessels shaped in baskets. Cedarbark and
other materials were used as binding materials. Following this, are observed experiments in firing and the use

of simple decorative designs in black upon a gray slip. This development is paralleled by the introduction of the bow and arrow and improvements in clothing and housing.

## THE PREHISTORIC PUEBLO BUILDERS

The periods known as Pueblo I, II, and III are wholly prehistoric, as was most of Pueblo IV, whose terminal years saw the initial phase of Spanish contact. Pueblo V is the historic period marked by increasing potency of European influence. Even though at first the Pueblo villagers were free to live their own lives, eventually, their cultural career was inhibited and the process of extinction and absorption into White cultures begun. To gain a general notion of what the prehistoric Pueblo culture was like some of its characteristics may be enumerated.

## BUILDINGS

The character of the ruins found in the Southwest, depended in part upon the period in which the buildings were constructed and in part upon the topography and other geographical conditions.

In widely separated localities are ruins of small partly subterranean structures with adobe walls supported by stone slabs around the base on the outside called slab houses. These houses were circular or oval, not rectangular, and appear to have had a conical roof of poles and thatch plastered with clay. The character and style of the pottery, as does stratigraphic evidence, indicate that these houses are older than the large community buildings and that they belonged to the forerunners of sedentary Pueblo peoples rather than to the ancestors of the nomadic tribes now living in the Southwest.

There are also widely scattered ruins consisting of houses of a few rooms (Pueblo II).  In the Mesa Verde region the rooms are arranged on three sides of a small plaza in which is a circular room nearly or quite underground.  An underground passageway from one of the

Square Watch Tower, San Juan River
(Courtesy of the late Dr. Prudden)

rooms of the house leads to this circular chamber, called a kiva by archaeologists.  That the buildings belonged to a period older than that in which large community houses were built is indicated by the crude masonry and the pottery which is less specialized.

Next come the large community houses usually of several terraced stories.

*Sites.* The building sites chosen by the prehistoric people seem to have depended in part upon the topog-

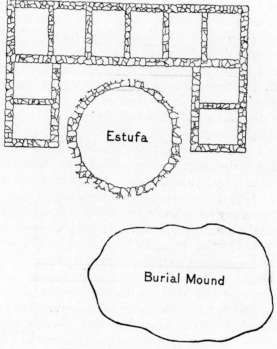

Diagram of Typical Small Ruin
(Courtesy of the late Dr. Prudden)

raphy of the particular locality and in part upon the need for defense. Few available caves seem to have been overlooked. The overhanging cliffs protected the structure from rain and most such situations were easily defended. The size of the buildings is of course limited

by the extent of the cave. Many of the pueblos were
built on the valley floors or on open plains, little thought
being given to the ease with which an enemy might
approach, but because of their peculiar arrangement
and construction such buildings were often easily defended. They were built either in the form of a
rectangle or a semicircle around a court from which
they were terraced back toward the outer wall which had
no openings low enough to be reached by the enemy.
Some of these, like Aztec on the Animas and Pueblo
Bonito in Chaco Canyon, had hundreds of rooms. A
great number of villages were placed on the tops of
mesas the walls of which were steep enough to furnish a
considerable degree of protection. Puyé, one of the
largest ruins on the Pajarito Plateau, is so situated.
In many instances a location was chosen just above the
head of a canyon, on the rim, at each side and at the
end of which the houses were built, making it impossible
for the enemy completely to surround the settlement.
In many places are ruins which from their character
and their location seem to have been built solely for
defense. These are round or square towers of considerable height which have a few small openings adapted
by their size and location for the observation of the
enemy and for the discharge of arrows. They were
usually placed to command a wide view of the surrounding country, often being perched on the top of a
boulder or block of stone.

*Materials.* The material employed in building apparently depended upon what was available in the
particular region. In the San Juan drainage sandstone was plentiful and not difficult to work and on the
Pajarito Plateau there was solidified volcanic ash, or
tufa, easy to cut. As a result, in both places there are
walls built of well-dressed blocks of stone. In other

Portion of Masonry Wall.  Chaco Canyon
(Courtesy of the late Dr. Prudden)

localities the stone is in thin strata and was broken off
and dressed only enough to smooth the surface of the
walls.  Where the walls were thick the two surfaces were
often well built and the intervening space filled roughly

Roof.   Spruce Tree Ruin
(Photo by Nusbaum)

Kiva at Spruce Tree Ruin
(Photo by Nusbaum)

with any available material. Some of the walls show regular courses of large stones alternating with courses of smaller ones producing a banded effect, evidently intentionally decorative.

Along the lower Gila and Salt rivers where bedrock as a source of building material was not available, round river boulders were used, the greater part of the walls being composed of adobe, the peculiar clay so abundant in the Southwest. The walls of the building known as Casa Grande were built of clay tempered with sand or gravel laid up in courses and each course allowed to harden before the next was laid. The clay appears to have been rich in lime which caused it to become very hard when thoroughly dry. Walls of the prehistoric pueblos of the Galisteo Basin have been found built of cubical blocks of adobe laid up without mortar.

The inner walls were almost always plastered and sometimes whitewashed and ornamented by painting. The impressions of the hands of the plasterers found here and there indicate that the women did that part of the work at least.

*Ceilings.* The ceilings and roofs of the rooms were made by placing round logs crosswise with their ends resting on or built into the walls. Above these were placed small poles much closer together and running in the opposite direction and on them a layer of small sticks and brush. A thick coating of wet clay was then applied and well packed down, probably by tramping it with the feet. This formed the ceiling and the roof or the ceiling and the floor of the story above, as the case might be.

*Doors.* The walls of the lower stories were usually without openings except small ones to admit light and air and through which one might look out. The larger openings in the upper portions of the walls were either rectangular or T-shaped and were raised a foot or two above the floor level, serving for both doors and windows. They were evidently reached by ladders and in some cases had balconies below them on which a landing from the ladders was made. These balconies were supported by the large ceiling timbers which were allowed to project beyond the walls for this purpose. The lower stories were reached by hatchways and ladders, either from the rooms above or from the roof, if the building was terraced.

*Kivas.* The kivas, peculiar rooms found in practically all the northern ruins, are, for the most part, circular and below ground and are ordinarily located in the courtyard. They vary greatly in size from ten or twelve feet to thirty or more feet in diameter. A firepit is usually found near the center and in most cases there is an airshaft of some size opening at the level of the floor and a masonry wall or stone slab in front of the opening to prevent a direct draft. It is not unusual to find masonry walls extending into the circular kivas for some feet, on which no doubt the timbered roof rested. They were evidently entered by hatchways through the roofs which consisted of timbers.

Within the range of the people who built the ruins in Chaco Canyon and the Aztec ruin, very large kivalike subterranean structures are found.

## Types of Ruins

*Cliff Palace.* The largest and perhaps best known cliff-dwelling is situated on Mesa Verde which is a few miles southwest of Mancos, Colorado. It has been named Cliff Palace and has been described by many writers since it was first mentioned in print about 1890. The cave which shelters it is 425 feet long, 80 feet wide in the middle, and reaches an extreme height of 80 feet. It occupies the eastern side of Cliff Palace Canyon, which is here about 200 feet deep. The cave opening, therefore, faces the west, with its axis roughly north and south. It resulted from the wearing away by the elements of a stratum of soft sandstone which was protected above by a harder layer that has remained to form the roof. Parts of the rock have broken from this roof and have fallen to the floor below where they have either remained or rolled out to form a sloping talus along its base. The floor of the cave as a result is very uneven, so that the structure stands upon four terraces of varying height with some of the rooms resting upon large blocks of stone.

It appears that it was not planned and built as a whole but that the first buildings were added to from time to time, both on the sides and above. The walls of this structure, which encloses 117 rooms, not counting those of the upper stories, were built of buff sandstone, well dressed and laid with adobe mortar in regular courses. The irregularities are chinked with stone fragments. The corners of the walls are not bonded nor are the joints of the stones regularly broken in the courses. It seems that these devices and that of the arch and its keystone were unknown to the ancient peoples. These walls, which are from one to two feet in thickness, were generally plastered on the inside and sometimes on the outside with a yellow mud laid on and smoothed with the hands, the prints of which are often plainly visible. In a few cases, the walls are ornamented with paintings.

Both rectangular and T-shaped doorways are found and several of them are provided with a recess in which slabs of stone were placed to close them.

Many of the ninety-four rooms which were evidently used for household purposes have fireplaces either in

one corner or in the center. The walls are blackened
with smoke for which no other exit was provided than
the doors and windows. In a few of the rooms there
is a raised bank along one side which may have furnished sleeping places. Certain rooms, especially those
with other rooms above them, show no signs of fire or
smoke and since they were entirely dark were without

Cliff

doubt used as storerooms for the food supply. A
number of rooms devoted to the grinding of corn have
boxes made of slabs of stone in which the grinding was
done on metates as at present in the Southwest. One
room has four such boxes side by side with the metates
still in place. There are many fireplaces in an open
plaza in the middle of the village, where much of the
cooking was probably done.

There are twenty-three kivas, situated in a court, most of them having their roofs level with the floors of the ordinary rooms of the first story. To give some of them the required depth the solid rock was excavated for several feet.

A round tower rising from the summit of a block of stone reaches the roof of the cave. It has been supposed

(Copyrighted by F. K. Vreeland)

Palace

that this served as a watch tower. It may have been that the whole structure was intended as a place in which the reserve food supply might be stored and defended, since in the neighborhood are ruins of other community structures in less easily defended situations.

*Spruce Tree House.* About two miles northwest in an adjoining canyon is another cave with a dwelling nearly as large and much better preserved. It is named Spruce Tree House from a tree found growing in the ruins which when cut in 1891 showed an age of 168 years. In this dwelling are several ceilings in a good state of preservation. This building and Cliff Palace were restored under the direction of the late Dr. J. W. Fewkes and it is expected that they will remain in this condition as permanent examples of such structures.

*Balcony House.* Not far from Cliff Palace and in the same canyon is Balcony House, so named because one of the balconies below the doors of an upper story was found intact by Nordenskiöld, who describes it as follows:

> The second story is furnished, along the wall mentioned, with a balcony; the joists between the two stories project a couple of feet, long poles lie across them parallel to the walls, the poles are covered with a layer of cedar bast and, finally, with dried clay. This balcony was used as a means of communication between the rooms in the upper story.

*Aztec.* The ruin called Aztec near the town of that name stands in an open valley. It is rectangular in shape with tiers of rooms on three sides. There are from five to seven rooms in width on the ground floor, and the outer row probably was originally four or five stories high, the walls of the ruin standing 29 feet above the foundation. The dimensions of the building are 359 by 280 feet enclosing a court 180 by 200 feet. The fourth side of this court was closed by a row of one-story rooms. There are remains of what was probably a rampart some yards distant which with the row of one-story rooms would have made the place easy to defend. From evidences observed it appears some parts of this structure were abandoned before others so that it is not probable that the entire building was occupied at one time. The excavation of the ruin was undertaken by the American Museum of Natural History in 1916

Aztec Ruin on the Las Animas, New Mexico
Above: General View before Excavation
Below: The Large Kiva in the Foreground and Repaired House Walls
to the Right

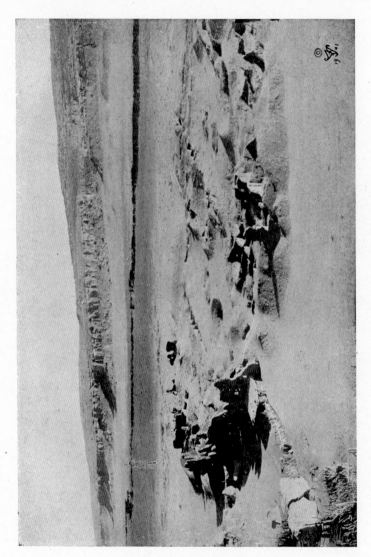

Pueblo Bonito Ruin

(Copyrighted by F. K. Vreeland)

44

and continued every summer until 1921. The walls have been reinforced with the expectation that the ruin will remain for years as a type of one of the larger community buildings unprotected by overhanging cliffs.

An examination of the pottery and the architecture indicates that the original builders and occupants were related to the Chaco Canyon people and that these were succeeded by a people with Mesa Verde affiliations. The large kiva is 41 feet in diameter and is surrounded by a line of small rooms on the ground level. The comparatively large space was roofed with timbers, remains of which were found during the excavation in a charred condition. While little is known of the purpose of these structures, they were evidently intended to hold a large group of people as audience or spectators. The only known purpose for bringing together large groups of people in the Southwest is to participate in or witness ceremonies, chiefly religious in character.

To ensure proper protection this Museum purchased a tract of land enclosing this and a number of adjoining ruins, donating them to the United States Government, which, in turn, created them a National Monument.

*Pueblo Bonito.* In Chaco Canyon stands a typical unprotected ruin of a large community house known as Pueblo Bonito. It is close to the north wall of the canyon, roughly semicircular in shape, with five or more rows of rooms on the ground, and was originally four or five stories high. Across the front was a double row of rooms one story high which enclosed a court, in which were twenty or more kivas. The entire length of the structure was 667 feet and its width 315 feet. It contained more than 500 rooms. The masonry of the walls varies in character, that of the first story being composed of medium-sized hewn stones and the upper stories of small flat stones faced to form the outer

surface. Many sticks of timber are included in the walls
to strengthen them. This ruin was excavated by the
Hyde Expedition of the American Museum in 1895–
1900 and many remarkable specimens were recovered.

Further excavation of this ruin as a National Monument was undertaken in 1921 by the National Geographic Society under the direction of Neil M. Judd
of the National Museum. It appears from the stratified
rubbish heap that the site has been occupied from very
early times.

*Cavate Lodges.* Along the Rio Grande and Rio
Verde are the simplest possible dwellings, those excavated in the soft rock walls of the canyons. It is
along the Rio Verde that the most elaborate of these
excavations are found. A round opening was made in
the face of the cliff for the door and sufficient rock
excavated to make a good-sized living room twelve feet
or more in its dimensions and high enough for one to
stand. Behind this were storerooms usually of less
size and height. There are hundreds of such rooms in
the canyon walls.

## MEANS OF SUSTENANCE

Agriculture furnished the main support. In the
Museum collections are specimens of corn on the ear, a
basket of shelled corn, and a bag of cornmeal. Beans
are also found, and squash and gourds are known to
have been raised.

We know little of their methods of tilling the land.
Their tools were simple wooden spatulas or small spades
of horn with wooden handles, with which the ground
was dug before and after the seed was planted. In much
of the territory occupied near the sources of the streams,
the valley lands were kept moist by the underflow and
did not require irrigation. At the elevation at which

these streams leave the mountains there is considerable rain in late summer, enough to mature corn even on the upland mesas. Near many of these mesa pueblos reservoirs are found which received the water from the mountain gulches and retained it for household purposes. In some cases the water thus impounded was used to irrigate the land. Near Solomonville on the upper portion of the Gila River the gardens were arranged in terraces on the sides and at the bases of the mountain slopes and were watered from reservoirs which retained the rain falling on the land above.

*Irrigation.* The people who occupied the valley of the Rio Verde in central Arizona made fairly extensive use of irrigation ditches in the watering of their crops. It is along the middle and lower courses of the Salt and Gila rivers that evidences are found of irrigation practised on a large scale. The Hemenway Archaeological Expedition, in 1887–1888, explored Los Muertos, a veritable city with thirty-six large communal structures, nine miles southeast of Tempe, Arizona. This ancient city, nine miles from the Salt River, was supplied with water by a large canal 7 ft. deep, 4 ft. wide at the bottom, and 30 ft. wide at the top. The walls and the bottom of the canal were very hard, as if they had been plastered with adobe clay after the soil had been thoroughly packed by tramping. It was suggested by the investigators that fires had been built in the canals and the clay baked by this means. Many side canals were provided for the distribution of the water over the fields. The posts of the gates for regulating the flow were found at the heads of these laterals. Mr. Hodge, who reported these excavations, estimates that similar canals provided for the irrigation of at least 200,000 acres, about half of the land in the valley available for agriculture. Recently some of these old canals have been cleaned out and they are again in use for irrigation purposes.

*Hunting.* The large number of bones of game animals found in the houses and refuse heaps indicates that hunting was not neglected. The weapons probably employed were bows and arrows, spears, and possibly clubs. The numerous pieces of large rope clearly show they had the means at hand for snares as well.

### MANUFACTURED OBJECTS

*Pottery.* One of the most characteristic arts of the Pueblo Dwellers was and still is the making of pottery. Besides the variety of objects of clay needed in the household at any definite time and place there must be considered the evolution in time of the art and the geographical distribution of various styles.

Prehistoric Coiled Ware

Black cooking vessels seem to be rather uniform over the entire area and to have been made and used at all periods. The vessels were no doubt built up by applying successive rounds of clay strips which were afterward pressed down and smoothed off until all traces of the separate pieces were obliterated. The black color probably resulted from smoke either when the vessel was being fired or while it was being used for cooking.

By leaving the filaments of clay unobliterated on the outside in a continuous spiral a pleasing texture was secured. In pressing down the fillet by applying the thumb with some attention to regularity and rhythm patterns were produced, sometimes highly decorative. This style of pottery, known as corrugated, is found over nearly all the Southwestern area. In the matter of time it has been shown that corrugated pottery began in Pueblo I, when the inhabitants of pit or slab houses used wide filaments about the upper portion of the vessels. It did not reach its finest stage until a fairly late period and continued to be made until about 1400. These vessels were used generally, perhaps solely, for cooking purposes. On the upper Gila a fine type of corrugated pottery, which seems to be of local origin rather than to belong to any definite period, has very narrow filaments of clay and is made with great skill. The interior of the vessels is highly polished.

For purposes other than cooking, another type of pottery known as black-on-white was used over the entire area, except the lower Gila, from the earliest times until the close of the Great (Pueblo III) Period. A white, or white modified to a gray or pink slip, is over the entire surface of the vessel, either inside or outside according to the exposure of the vessel to view. On this white surface designs in black were painted. The black-on-white pottery made by the builders of the slab houses and of the small houses was decidedly inferior to that which is found in connection with the large community houses. Those who are familiar with the pottery of this sort from the various parts of the Southwest are able to tell at a glance from what

region a vessel comes. From Mesa Verde are flat
bottomed mugs with handles. Vessels from this region
frequently have black dots on the edge of the rim.
From Pueblo Bonito come tall, cylindrical vessels
some of which have realistic designs. From the very

Tularosa Pottery

headwaters of the Gila River have been secured collections showing a great variety of forms and styles of
decoration, some of which are definitely characteristic
of the region. South, along the Mimbres, has been
excavated a large number of beautiful and curious

vessels, many of them having for designs finely executed animal and human figures.

Pottery with a red surface on which designs are painted in black occurs generally in the Southwest, but

Pueblo Bonito Pottery

Prehistoric Pottery.   Lower Gila River
(Courtesy of Peabody Museum)

in the Little Colorado drainage is a ware with a red slip on which the heavier designs are painted in black, with narrower lines in white, which often border the black figures.  This Little Colorado region is especially noted for a buff ware on which designs are painted in black which are also often bordered with white.

Rather late in the pre-Spanish period (Pueblo IV), over a large area centering in the Santa Fé region, a glaze paint was applied to a red or gray surface. At about the beginning of the Spanish occupation the glaze was combined with paint on the same vessels. Soon after the art of using the glaze began to deteriorate and the modern painted ware made its appearance.

*Baskets.* Since baskets, bags, and sandals are conspicuous in all Basket Maker collections a brief description seems desirable. The better baskets are sewed on a coiled foundation. This foundation consists of two small peeled rods, placed side by side. Above them is placed a small bundle of fibers, a few splints, or sometimes only two splints or welts. The sewing stitches pass through this bundle or between these splints so as to enclose a part of them and tie the successive coils together. The stitches do not ordinarily interlock. The specimens which have been preserved indicate a fair degree of skill and technical ability. The surviving material is too scanty to furnish a basis for a knowledge of the character or the variety of their designs. One of the common types of basketry of Pueblo times consists of a diagonal plaiting of strips of yucca leaves attached to a heavy wooden withe which forms the border.

In addition, there are many types of soft bag, woven of yucca fiber strings, usually with banded decoration.

*Sandals.* The sandals, of which there is a long series in the Museum collections, chiefly Basket Maker Period, show great variety in the methods employed in making them and in their ornamentation. The simpler ones are diagonally plaited with broad strips

of yucca leaves. Others are twined with two strands
and usually have the lower side thickened and cush-
ioned by imbrication or the attachment of additional

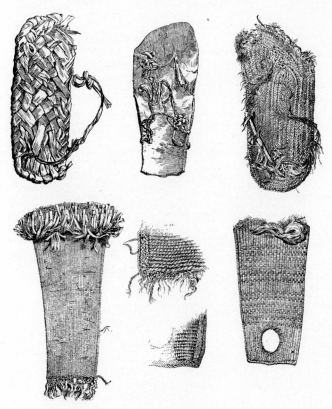

Types of Prehistoric Sandals

material in the form of numerous loops or rows of
twine. The warp is usually of coarse stiff fibers,
probably derived from yucca leaves, but the woof
appears to be of apocynum fiber. The designs in red

Yucca Fiber Bag.    Grand Gulch

and black are usually arranged in horizontal stripes and bands.

*Textiles.* The introduction of cotton gave the early Pueblo peoples a much better fiber and so we find good cotton cloth in our collections. The cotton was most probably raised in the locality where it was used. No complete looms used in cloth-making have as yet been recovered, but minor implements have been found. These include forks and batten sticks, both being implements used in pressing down the warp. In the floor of certain kivas places have been found where it is supposed looms were attached. It is altogether probable the loom was of the general type still used by the Pueblo Indians. This form is common along the Pacific drainage of America south to Chile.

A most interesting piece of weaving is a small robe or kilt found wrapped around a body. The weaving is diagonal, producing raised patterns which are further accentuated by the use of black, red, and yellow dye. This is probably the finest piece of textile work known from the Southwest (illustrated on page 60).

Dating from the last ancient occupation of Canyon del Muerto, a unique mummy bundle discovered in 1929, offers added evidence of the weaver's art. The body was found in a masonry crypt in the floor of a cave and was accompanied by numerous perfectly preserved objects. The outer wrapping of the body is a fine feather blanket about which are many hanks of elaborately wound cotton yarn of varying sizes, the strands of which have a total length of over two miles. The inner wrapping consists of two plain white cotton blankets and the wrist and left hand are firmly bound with cotton cloth and a strip of soft buckskin.

While the specimens recovered from the northwestern portion of the area indicate a great variety and perfection in textile art, there are many examples of cotton and yucca fiber textiles from all parts of the area.

*Stonework.* The grinding stones employed were metates of the same sort now used in the Southwest and found in the southern portion of California, in Mexico and Central America, and generally in South America. The bottom stone, the metate, is a slab roughened by pecking and often ground down in the middle so that it has a raised border on either side. For use, it has the front end raised, making an angle of about 30 degrees with the floor. The upper stone, called a mano, is usually a rectangular prism which is grasped at both ends by the hands of a kneeling woman and rubbed up and down over the bottom stone.

The axes and pestles, made by pecking and grinding selected stones, are gracefully shaped and excellently made. The usual method of attaching a handle to the ax was to wrap a stout withe around it in the one or more grooves provided.

The flaked objects of jasper and flint show excellent workmanship and many of them are very pleasing in outline. There are many arrowheads and drill points and a few large pieces which were evidently used on spears. Some of the arrows are of reeds with foreshafts while others have simple shafts. The drills are also simple and arrow-like. The fire-making apparatus is represented by several large fragments of the hearth or bottom piece and drills, some of which are compound like a foreshafted arrow.

A great variety of objects made of stone, shell, and bone has been secured. Some of the most interesting of these are exceedingly small stone disk beads with minute perforations drilled for stringing. Very beautiful inlaid work has been recovered, pieces of turquoise being set in jet or bone to form mosaics. The wonderful deposits of turquoise obtained at Pueblo Bonito by the Hyde Expedition illustrate both the ability and the aesthetic taste of these early inhabitants of the Southwest. There are thousands of disk-shaped, perforated turquoise beads, rectangular pieces which seem to have been fastened to the clothing, splendidly carved

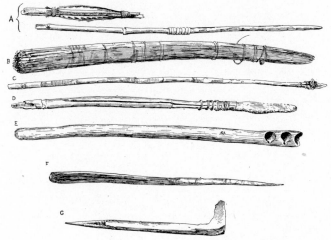

Objects of Wood and Bone, *a*, Arrow; *b*, Sinew-wrapped End of Bow; *c*, Flint-pointed Drill; *d-e*, Firedrill; *f*, Wooden Awl; *g*, Bone Awl.

birds and insects, and remarkable mosaics. As examples of the latter may be mentioned a cylinder the core of which had largely disintegrated but with the mosaic covering still left in position, a bone scraper with an inlaid band, and a frog of jet with necklace and eyes of inlaid turquoise.

At Pueblo Bonito were also found several flageolets, some of them decorated with painted designs, and one or two with carved figures of birds. From

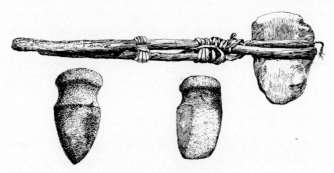

Stone Axes and Hammers

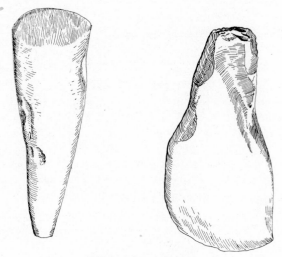

Polished Stone Chisels

Grand Gulch there are a rattle of small hoofs of deer or antelope and also some dice, together with a cup from which they may have been thrown.

There is no reason to suppose that the prehistoric peoples of the Southwest knew how to secure and make use of the copper which is abundant in that region. A few pieces of copper in the form of bells and orna-

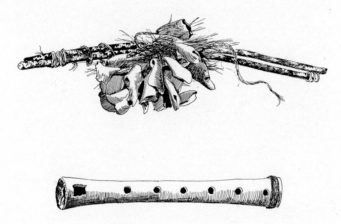

Prehistoric Rattle and Flageolet

ments were found at Pueblo Bonito but it is more than likely they were brought from Mexico in trade. Some remarkable fragments of stones, pottery and basketry covered with cloisonné work are believed to have reached Pueblo Bonito in the same manner.

## DISPOSAL OF DEAD

The dead were variously disposed of. In the northwest along Grand Gulch and Cottonwood Creek they were buried in caves and under the floors of houses.

In several parts of the Southwest the bodies of children received special treatment, being enclosed in the masonry walls or under the floors of houses. The adults are generally found in cemeteries in the neighborhood

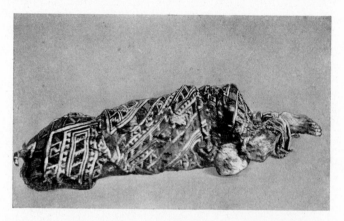

Mummy Wrapped in a Cotton Robe. Grand Gulch, Utah

of the pueblo and even in the rubbish heaps. Along the lower Gila at one period cremation and the burial of the ashes in urns were practised.

## RELIGION

We know little of the religious practices in prehistoric times. There are many objects which may with reason be supposed to have been ceremonial in their use. In the Rio Grande region are found large stone images that have long been supposed to be idols. Mr. N. C. Nelson, while excavating Pueblo Largo ruin in Galisteo Valley, found a stone image before which on a raised adobe platform were several pottery vessels and queerly shaped stones. These objects and their arrangement certainly present an early type of the altar still in use among the Pueblo Indians.

## SUMMARY

Perhaps nowhere in North America is it possible to reconstruct so detailed and vivid a picture of the life of a prehistoric people as in the Southwest. The generally arid climate and the protection of large caves have preserved textiles and other objects which usually disintegrates.

The large community houses of the Pueblo Period brought together considerable numbers of people who lived together in close association. Such communities subdivided no doubt into small groups on the basis of relationship, wealth, or ceremonial and religious duties. We must assume rulers or officers both political and religious. They were of necessity an industrious people since considerable tracts of land were planted each year to corn, beans, squash, and probably cotton. In addition, considerable quantities of wild grass seeds, nuts, and similar food were gathered. There are evidences that flocks of turkeys proportional to the needs of each settlement were kept and that they were given proper care and housing. We do not know that their flesh was used for food but their feathers were in great demand for clothing. A certain amount of hunting was also done, for the bones found indicate that deer and lesser animals were used for food.

The food of course had to be prepared and served. Each woman probably made her own dishes of clay. Such skill and art as are displayed in the pottery of the Southwest are not easily acquired. The girls must have been educated by frequent instruction and practice in the art. Clothing seems to have been made by the time consuming methods of hand manufacture: the preparation of the fibers, either of cotton or yucca, spinning by hand, and the slow building up of a web of cloth by adding thread to thread in a primitive loom. The houses needed a certain amount of care, especially those built in the open places. The roofs had to be kept tight and the walls plastered and protected from rain. In some instances there seems to have been constant addition of rooms to these community structures. In other cases the entire population moved away and built again.

With all this busy industrial life we know there was time for the making of many ornaments, and there are reasons to believe that games and sports were engaged in and that ceremonies of some sort were performed.

In short, life was not particularly different from that observed in the Southwest later by the Spaniards and which may still be witnessed at Zuñi and on the Hopi mesas. It may be added that in contrast with the North American Indians in general, the daily life in these regions was not strikingly different from that in agricultural village communities in Europe at the same period. The more essential differences were the lack of domestic animals which assisted the European peasant in his labors and the limited commerce in America.

According to our present information we must consider that the inhabitants of these cliff ruins and the ruined community houses which are scattered over the Southwest are the ancestors of the present-day Pueblo people. Certainly the culture they developed has survived, on the Rio Grande, at Zuñi, and on the Hopi mesas with no great amount of change. Whether the Basket Makers were the direct ancestors of the Pueblo Dwellers, is to be doubted. The marked change in head form strongly suggests the infusion of new Indian blood, but that culture influences were passed on from Basket Maker to Pueblo time is clear. Whether a still more nomadic mode of life preceded Basket Maker we do not know.

# Chapter II

# THE PUEBLO DWELLERS

## Exploration

During the first half of the sixteenth century the rule of Spain was being extended beyond the Valley of Mexico by the successors of Cortez. In particular, the Gulf of California was being explored and its eastern shore was being organized into the province of New Galicia. To take possession of the region about the mouth of the Rio Grande, Narvaez, with a considerable company, had sailed from Cuba, but was forced by a storm to land on the west coast of Florida. The party made their way painfully toward the west finally building some small vessels in which they attempted to sail to their destination.

*Cabeza de Vaca.* Eight years later, in 1536, the treasurer of this ill-fated expedition, Cabeza de Vaca, with two Spaniards and a negro named Estevan, arrived in New Galicia, having crossed Texas and northern Mexico on foot. They brought reports of great "cows" on which the natives of the vast plains lived and also accounts of settled towns. The ancient Mexicans had a myth which told of their origin in the north where there were seven caves or seven canyons from which they believed they had migrated. There were rumors also in Mexico of seven cities of great wealth in the north. This was an adventurous age and men were looking for new lands where gold already mined was to be obtained, and where there were men to be converted if possible or slain if necessary.

*Marcos de Niza.* A Franciscan friar, Marcos de Niza, was sent with the negro, Estevan, as guide and a small escort of troops to investigate this report of the seven cities to the north. As they journeyed to the north they heard continually of great and rich cities, but to the Europeans acquainted with Mexico and Peru great and rich meant one thing and to the natives quite another.

When they reached Vacapa, in central Sonora, Estevan was directed to go in advance to search out the best route. He was ordered to send back word of what he might find and not to proceed more than fifty or sixty leagues. Estevan sent back messengers, but hastened on himself. After waiting for some days the friar followed. A month later, when he had reached the mountainous country, he was met by one of the men who had been with the negro, and told that the advance party had reached the seven cities but that Estevan had been killed by the natives. Friar Marcos went on until in the distance he could see one of the villages of the Zuñi Indians, probably Hawikuh, and was then forced by his unwilling followers to return.

*Coronado.* The report that Friar Marcos brought back was sufficiently glowing to inspire an expedition the next year under the leadership of Francisco Vazquez Coronado, who had been made governor of New Galicia. He had as his chief lieutenant, Hernando de Alvarado. The advance guard arrived at Cibola, the name given to the former villages of the Zuñi, on July 7, 1540. There was some fighting during which Coronado was wounded and after which the Indians took refuge on Thunder Mountain, surrendering their villages to the Spaniards. Don Pedro de Tovar was sent to investigate the report of seven other cities to the northwest. He visited the Hopi villages in the region known to the Spaniards as Tusayan and returned bringing an account of the villages and of a great river to the west with a deep uncrossable canyon.

Alvarado, the second in command, was sent with a few men to explore toward the east. He passed a high mesa on which was perched the village of Acoma, and arrived at the Rio Grande, probably near Bernalillo, where he found villages similar to those of Cibola. Coronado joined him there with the main army passing the winter in one of the villages. The natives, who were at first friendly, being offended by the constant demands for food and clothing and by the ill treatment of their women, drove off the horses and mules of the Spaniards. The village responsible for this was attacked and some of the men surrendered. When these prisoners observed the officer in charge having two hundred stakes prepared to which the Indians were to be tied and roasted alive, they seized the stakes and renewed the fight. In the end they were all killed, but their deaths were no doubt somewhat more agreeable. During the winter the country along the Rio Grande was explored to the north and south, and the various villages seen were enumerated and described. In one of these villages was a captive from among the Plains Indians, an Indian called by the Spaniards, the Turk, who told of a still more wonderful country to the east called Quivira.

The next spring a part of the invaders started to visit this country, taking Turk as their guide. They soon reached the open country, east of the mountains, where they encountered vast herds of buffalo, "the cows" reported by de Vaca. Following these herds were Indians who had skin tents which they transported with the aid of dogs. After traveling for some weeks, evidently in the wrong direction, being deceived by Turk, another Indian led them to some unimportant villages of agricultural Indians. The distances and directions given in the narratives would have brought them to some part of eastern Kansas. After staying there twenty-five days they returned to the Rio Grande, where they spent the winter, during which Coronado fell from his horse and was seriously hurt. A council was held which decided upon an immediate return to Mexico, whither they all set out gladly except two monks, who chose to remain behind and preach to the Indians. They soon perished, however, at the hands of the natives. The expectations of those who had organized the expedition had been great. They were looking for another Mexico or Peru with great cities and accompanying wealth, but nothing seemed to have resulted from the expedition worth the labor and expense involved.

## The Conquest

Forty years later, in 1508, Francisco Sanchez Chamuscado, accompanied by three Franciscan missionaries, went up the Rio Grande to New Mexico, and left them there to begin the Christianizing of the Indians. All three were killed during the following winter. When their fate was known in Mexico, Antonio de Espejo, with fourteen Spaniards, visited the principal pueblos. Upon his return his report resulted in so much interest that Juan de Oñate was allowed to colonize the country. In 1598 he came to New Mexico with one hundred and thirty white men and many Indians, visited the important pueblos, received their submission, and established a capital at Chamita, where the Rio Chama flows into the Rio Grande. Here the first church, San Gabriel, was built. De Oñate continued as governor until 1608. At about that time the capital was transferred to Santa Fé. By 1630 most of the villages were provided with churches and missionaries.

## The Rebellion

The natives, vassals of the king of Spain, were treated harshly by the civil and military authorities; the priests, eager to establish their religion, forced it upon the Indians, at the same time repressing the native beliefs and practices. These two causes produced a feeling of resentment which finally resulted in rebellion in 1680. The heads of the Pueblos communicated with each other and appointed a day on which all the white people should be killed. One of the inhabitants of San Juan was kindly disposed toward the rulers and priests and gave them warning, but this only resulted in an immediate attack in which the priests in all the near by villages were killed. Word was sent to the other villages of the miscarriage of the plot and the priests and Spaniards living in them were killed. Governor Otermin, after several days of unsuccessful fighting about Santa Fé which had become the capital, fled to El Paso with many of the Spanish inhabitants. He returned the next year and succeeded in capturing Isleta, but failed to reëstablish his rule.

In 1683 Petriz de Cruzat became governor. He was later removed and still later reappointed. He made a successful march as far as Sia where in an all-day battle he beat the combined Indians, killing 600 and capturing 70 of them. Before the report of this victory reached the king, Don Diego de Vargas was appointed as his successor. He conducted a vigorous campaign from 1692 until 1696, during which he tried in vain to take the Black Mesa near Española upon which the inhabitants of San Ildefonso had established themselves, but succeeded in capturing Old Cochiti in a night attack. Most of the warriors had escaped, and by a counter attack they released half of the 340 women and children

held as prisoners.  De Vargas burned the village and
took the stored corn to Santa Fé.  In the end the
Indians were subjugated and peace was established,
and thereafter they were not again treated so harshly.
The priests became more tolerant toward the native
religious practices and less insistent upon anything but a
nominal acceptance of Christianity.


## Distribution in 1540

If we assume that all the inhabited pueblos, with one
exception mentioned below, were seen by members of
Coronado's party, it appears that there had already
been a considerable shrinkage in the Pueblo area.
They did not hear of villages anywhere on the San Juan
or Gila rivers or their tributaries.  With the Coronado
expedition was a private soldier interested in ethnology,
Pedro de Castañeda, left not only a most readable
narrative of the journey itself, but interesting observations concerning the number and location of villages
and the manner of life of the natives.  He listed the
villages and described them as located in the following
provinces:

*Cibola.*  This province when first discovered was
said to have seven villages.  Of these the location of
five seems fairly certain.  They are Hawikuh and Ket-
tcippawa near Ojo Caliente, the present Zuñi, then
known as Halona, and Matsaki and Kiakima near
Thunder Mountain.  At the time of the rebellion in
1680 Hawikuh, Zuñi, Matsaki, and Kiakima were still
inhabited.  At the close of the rebellion the people
gathered at Zuñi where they remained until the recent
movement to the outlying districts.

*Tusayan.*  The province of Tusayan also had seven
villages situated near the sites of the present Hopi

pueblos. One of the most important of these, Awatobi, because it received a missionary after the rebellion, was attacked by the other Hopi people in 1700 and was abandoned. At about the same time Hano, near Walpi, on the first mesa, was settled by Indians who came from pueblos on the Rio Grande. Castañeda estimated the population of the two provinces of Cibola and Tusayan at between three and four thousand.

*Acoma.* The high mesa with Acoma on its top, reached by difficult trails, is unmistakably described. The cisterns on the mesa which hold the rain and melted snow are mentioned. The population is given as two hundred men.

*Tiguex.* The province of Tiguex, on the Rio Grande near Bernalillo, had twelve villages scattered along the valley on either side of the river. None of these villages is now inhabited. Along the river was the province of Tutahaco with eight villages, probably in the neighborhood of Isleta which may occupy the site of one of them. Still farther down the Rio Grande were three villages which may have been situated as far south as San Marcial, where there are ruins of the former Piro villages.

*Salinas.* East of the river were at least three villages not mentioned by any of Coronado's followers but included later in the district of Salinas, named from the salt lakes in the neighborhood. These villages of Abo, Quarai, and Tabira, generally known as Gran Quivira, were hard pressed by the Apache and appear to have been deserted about 1675. When Governor Otermin passed down the Rio Grande in 1680 after the uprising, the inhabitants of the villages on the lower Rio Grande, Socorro, Sevilleta, and Alamillo, collectively known as the Piro, then few in number from the raids of the Apache, joined him. They were left

near El Paso where a few of their descendants are still
living at Isleta del Sur.

*Quirix.* Just north of Tiguex was the province of
Quirix with seven villages, probably those now represented by the Keresan villages of Santo Domingo, San
Felipe, Santa Ana, Sia, and Cochiti, the location of,
many of which was changed during the rebellion.

Pueblo of Walpi
(Photo by Howard McCormick)

*Tanos.* To the east of these, was Ximena, with three
villages in Galisteo Valley, deserted at the time of the
rebellion. These Galisteo pueblos were excavated for
the American Museum during the summer of 1912 by
Mr. N. C. Nelson. In the "snowy mountains" there
were seven villages, not referred to by name, now completely in ruins and hard to identify.

*Cicuye.* On the Pecos River was the one large pueblo known to the followers of Coronado as Cicuye. It was estimated at that time to contain 500 fighting men. The population of Pecos slowly decreased, room after room of the great pueblo being abandoned, until in 1838 the handful of survivors moved to Jemez.

Pueblo of Zuñi
(Copyrighted by Fred Harvey)

This ruined village has been excavated by Phillips Academy under the direction of Dr. A. V. Kidder.

*Jemez.* The province given the name of Hemes by Castañeda, consisted in his time of seven villages with three additional ones at Aguas Calientes, Jemez Hot Springs. The population was concentrated during the seventeenth century until only two of these villages were occupied. After the rebellion, during which Jemez suffered particularly, only one village was maintained.    Many of the inhabitants fled to the Navajo among whom their descendants form a clan.

*Tewa.*   Northward was Yuqueyunque, at the mouth of the Chama and six villages in the mountains which probably included the pueblos north of Santa Fé. Finally, several leagues to the north, were the two pueblos of Picuris and Taos, the latter called Braba, both located nearly as they stand today.

Besides these inhabited villages, others are mentioned as having been recently destroyed by a Plains tribe called by the Spaniards, Teya, possibly the Comanche.

Castañeda summarizes the Rio Grande region with a statement that these sixty-six villages were scattered over a distance of 130 leagues having the province of Tiguex near the middle with a combined population of 20,000 men.

Judging from the ruins, it appears that the area inhabited by sedentary peoples had been reduced to nearly a half at the time the Spaniards first entered the country and the number of inhabited villages today is much smaller than when Coronado visited them in 1540.   Pecos, the pueblos of the Galisteo Valley, and of the Salinas District, and all those on the Rio Grande south of Isleta are in ruins.

Not more than one or two of the pueblos are situated exactly as they were in 1540.   Immediately after the rebellion, the pueblos in the less easily defended situations were deserted and others were built in more secure locations.   The inhabitants of San Ildefonso took refuge on the top of Black Mesa; those of Cochiti left their village on the slope of the mesa and built another on the top, where they were joined by refugees from other pueblos.   Nearly all the Hopi villages were also moved at that time to the tops of the mesas.   The inhabitants of Zuñi went to the top of Thunder Mountain. Although some of the pueblos were captured by the Spaniards and certain abandoned pueblos were burned during the re-conquest, most of the changes in location seem to have been made voluntarily in anticipation of Spanish vengeance.

## PRESENT DISTRIBUTION

*Rio Grande.* The villages now occupied are usually separated into three groups, the Rio Grande, the Hopi pueblos, and Zuñi. The Rio Grande pueblos are again divided into the Tanoan and Keresan, because the languages of the two groups are totally different. There are also minor differences in culture. The Tanoan group consists of Taos, Picuris, San Juan, Santa Clara, San Ildefonso, Tesuque, Pojoaque, Nambe, Jemez, Sandia, and Isleta. Those which speak the Keresan language are San Felipe, Cochiti, Santo Domingo, Santa Ana, Sia, Laguna, and Acoma.

*Hopi.* The Hopi villages are geographically separated into the first or eastern mesa on which stand Walpi, Sichumovi, and Hano; the second or middle mesa with Shipaulovi, Mishongnovi, Shumopovi; and on the third mesa, Oraibi and Hotavila. The latter was founded a few years ago by the conservative party of Oraibi who wished to maintain old ways and to avoid sending their children to the government school. Forty miles westward is the summer village of Moenkapi situated where conditions are exceptionally favorable to agriculture. The language of the Hopi proper is Shoshonean, connected with Ute and Comanche. However, one of the villages, Hano, still has its Tewan dialect, maintained since the migration from the Rio Grande early in the eighteenth century.

*Zuñi.* The pueblo of Zuñi, the descendant of the seven cities of Cibola, has three outlying farming villages, Pescado, Nutria, and Ojo Caliente which are fast becoming permanent settlements. The Zuñi language is believed to be entirely independent of all others.

## HABITATIONS

The houses of the sedentary peoples of the Southwest retain the chief characteristics of those of the ancient peoples which are really the most striking features of Southwestern culture: they are communal, honeycomb-like, and almost without exception, terraced.

*Arrangement of Buildings.* The modern villages present three types of arrangement. A large square or rectangular building, terraced back from all four sides, results in a pyramid which is easily defended. The common prehistoric arrangement around an enclosed court from which the upper stories recede is still found. The third type has the houses in long parallel rows terraced back from the streets.

In the Rio Grande region Taos has two large houses of the pyramidal type situated on either side of a beautiful stream. One of these is five and the other four stories high. San Ildefonso, Jemez, Santa Clara, and San Felipe have one or more enclosed courts. Acoma is an excellent example of the third type having three rows of three-story houses, terraced back from the streets. Santo Domingo and San Juan have a similar arrangement.

Zuñi combines both the first and second types of arrangement. It is terraced back from the outside but also has several courts, in the largest of which the old church is situated. The pueblo is intersected by a number of passageways or streets leading to the interior.

A study of the village of Zuñi brings out the interesting fact that the same general arrangement and the lines of the village have been maintained for many years practically unchanged while many of the individual houses and house walls have been altered and replaced.

It is on the Hopi mesas that structures more like those of prehistoric and early Spanish times are found.

Floor Plan of Hopi Living Room
(After Cosmos Mindeleff)

One of the smaller pueblos, Shipaulovi, is built about a square court from which it is terraced back and upon which the lower terrace has its openings. Several of the other pueblos show signs of having been first built around a court and then added to as the inhabitants grew in numbers until there are now several courts. Mishongnovi has three completed ones and the beginning of another. Shumopovi has one well-enclosed court and another partly enclosed, but the houses are terraced to face the east. At Walpi, which has grown until it has nearly covered all the available space, the older portion of the building surrounds a court from which it is terraced back. Oraibi is arranged in long irregular rows.

*Building Material.* The pueblos of the Rio Grande region are largely built of adobe brick, the art of making which was fairly certainly learned from the natives of Mexico who came into the Southwest with Oñate and later. Clay, first mixed with straw and water, is molded in rectangular forms and allowed to dry in the sun. These bricks are laid in regular courses with similar material for mortar. Such walls are durable only when they are protected from rain by means of extended roofs, or by constant plastering.

Castañeda gives a description of the older method of preparing adobe. He says fires were made of small brush and sedge-grass upon which, when the sticks were falling to ashes, water and clay were thrown. The material was then molded into balls and laid like stones in courses with mortar of similar material. He tells us that this masonry work was performed by the women, but that the men did the carpenter work, preparing the timbers and putting them into place. The inner walls were plastered and sometimes painted, but he does not tell us what material was used. At the present time burned gypsum is employed as a white-wash, but this method has probably been adopted from the Mexicans who also use it.

Acoma is built of rubble and clay. A village in the same situation as the present one and probably the one described by several of Coronado's party, was partly burned in 1599. The village was not destroyed during the rebellion a century later, and the walls now in use may be the same seen in 1540, repaired and in part rebuilt from time to time.

While Zuñi is built mostly of adobe, the cornices frequently have several courses of flat stones.

The Hopi houses are built of stone poorly dressed and poorly laid as compared with the best prehistoric masonry. Mindeleff, who published a splendid account of Pueblo architecture, observed women building a detached house with the help of one man who lifted the timbers into place. While the men are said to build the walls sometimes, the women are always expected to do the plastering. The ceilings are made in the prehistoric fashion with beams, cross poles, brush, and clay spread over all and tramped down. The floors are sometimes flagged with large flat stones. The walls inside are generally whitened with gypsum and sometimes ornamented by leaving unwhitened bands at top and bottom. The fireplaces situated in one corner of the room are provided with hoods which receive the smoke and communicate with chimneys which are generally topped with a pot or two from which the bottom has been broken. In another corner of the room is generally found the three-sectioned milling box with three grinding stones. Many of the rooms of the lower terrace are used for storage.

A few T-shaped doorways like those found in prehistoric ruins may still be seen in the Hopi houses. During the Spanish period windows in the walls were more generally used. They were covered with thin sheets of selenite which was the substitute for glass in general use in the Southwest. Ordinary windows and hinged doors are now in common use.

## SHELTERS

To shelter those who are to tend the crops and as a camping place for the family when the fields are far from the village, temporary structures are built. The common type is made by setting four posts at the corners of a rectangle so that their forked tops are seven or eight feet above the ground. These posts support a platform of poles and brush which casts a shade and furnishes on its top a storage place away from dogs and stray animals. The Hopi often cut trees or brush and set them in curved or straight lines so as to break the wind and furnish the desired shade. The two forms are sometimes combined so that the space under the platform has a wall of brush on one side. Temporary rectangular houses of stone with flat roofs are also built by the Hopi and Zuñi.

## KIVAS

The modern pueblos, with a few exceptions, are each provided with one or more kivas. In a general way, they resemble the prehistoric kivas, both in their structure and their location.

The kivas of the Rio Grande region are frequently circular, the roofs of some of them being level with the ground while others are built up to a considerable height so that their forms are readily apparent from the outside. Details as to their structure are not available except that they are entered through hatchways by means of ladders which project to a considerable height. With the exception of the fireplace, the ladder, and the posts supporting the two main roof beams, they are said to be entirely without furnishings. The Keresan kivas, of which there are always two to a village, known as the summer and winter kivas, are said in some instances to be permanently decorated with the pictures of the animals associated in mythology and ceremonies with the cardinal points. The kivas of San Juan and Santa Clara are rectangular and above ground and those of Jemez and Acoma are included in the regu-

Kiva.   San Ildefonso
(Copyrighted by Fred Harvey)

lar house structure differing externally from ordinary rooms only in the projection of ladder tops.

At Hopi they are frequently built in the side of the mesa so that the wall of the kiva on one side is exposed to light and air while the roof is still kept level with the surface of the mesa. They are all rectangular, about twenty-five feet long and half as broad. The floor, which is generally paved with stone, is in two levels. The higher portion, a foot above the other,

occupies about one third the entire floor space. This
is reserved for spectators. In the lower part is a
fireplace, a mere rectangular pit placed in the center
directly under the hatchway; and at one end there is a
small cavity covered by a plank in which a hole is cut,
furnished with a close fitting plug. This represents
the lower world and the place of emergence through
which the people and animals originally came to this
world, and through it the deities are now supposed to

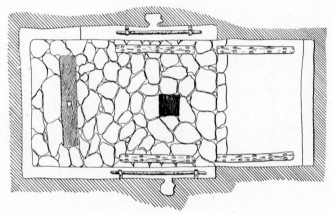

Floor Plan of Hopi Kiva
(After Victor Mindeleff)

come during the ceremonies. Along the sides of the
room are placed slabs provided with holes to receive
the posts of the looms which are usually set up and used
in the kivas. Sometimes a stone-capped bench along
one or more of the side walls provides seats. At the
farther end of the lower level a similar bench about
two feet high is used as a shelf on which images are
placed; and an opening in front holds certain masks
when they are not in use.

The walls, which are of stone, are kept nicely plastered by the women. The roof is composed first of large logs placed crosswise resting on top of the two side walls; next, of many smaller poles placed lengthwise which in turn are covered with brush and well packed clay. In the middle a space about five feet by seven is left for the hatchway. Masonry walls resting on the ceiling beams are carried up for a few feet on all four sides. Across the top of these walls are laid planks leav-

Roof of Hopi Kiva
(After Victor Mindeleff)

ing an opening four and a half feet long and two feet wide. Through this hatchway a ladder top projects ten or twelve feet.

At Zuñi there are six ceremonial rooms known as *kiwwitsiwe* where the masked men who represent the gods in the ceremonies meet and rehearse. These, located in various parts of the town proper, are not underground, and do not have the prescribed form and structure which characterize the circular kivas of the Rio Grande or the rectangular ones of the Hopi.

Castañeda and other early Spanish writers seem to have been amused by these kivas—"estufas" (stoves) they called them.  They are described as being situated in the yards of the buildings with their roofs level with the ground.  There were in that day both square and round kivas.  Those of Taos are mentioned, in particular; one was said to have twelve pine posts of large size supporting the roof.  The floors were paved with large smooth stones with a boxed-in fireplace in which small brush was burned for heat, enabling the occupants to remain in them as in a bath.

The kivas today are used as clubrooms and lounging places as well as workshops, the weaving usually being done in them.  They are chiefly, however, more or less sacred rooms set apart for ceremonial purposes.  In them are held those portions of the ceremonies which it is desired to keep secret from the uninitiated public.  They also serve as places of retreat for those who, for a time, must avoid profane contaminations.


## FOOD

The method of securing food is always the central fact in a people's existence around which social life, art, and religion are largely built.  There are considerable regions in North America where agriculture was not practised.  In the great plains the chief dependence was upon the buffalo, while on the North Pacific Coast the people lived largely on fish.  The inhabitants of the Plateau area lived upon wild vegetables, small game, and insects.  The sedentary peoples of the Southwest placed their main reliance on the crops which their fields produced.  These were in earlier times, corn, beans, and squash.  Recently wheat and other small grains and vegetables have been added.  Hunting was by no means neglected for flesh was needed to produce a balanced diet. The wild vegetables in the neighborhood were gathered and preserved for later use.

*Agriculture.* The fields of the Rio Grande peoples are situated in the river bottoms and along the smaller streams near their villages. Irrigation is now practised and was being practised at many of the pueblos, when the Spaniards first arrived. There were however no great difficulties involved, and no large canals like the prehistoric ones of the lower Salt River were necessary. The fields of the Acoma are fourteen miles away at Acomita and Pueblito, apparently where they were when Espejo visited them in 1583. He mentions both the cornfields two leagues away, and the river from which he says they watered them.

The Hopi fields are situated near the mesas wherever there is sufficient moisture from some gulch or spring. Corn is planted ten or twelve inches deep with a planting stick which makes a suitable hole. The corn is not raised in rows, but in large clumps of eight or ten stalks, at considerable distances from each other. While the plants are young, they are protected from the wind and the drifting sand by windbreaks of brush or stone. Irrigation is not practised except that vegetables are sometimes watered by hand. Ditches, however, are provided to carry off the excessive fall of water during heavy showers.

Because of the large population of Zuñi many of their fields are at a great distance; the people move in large numbers to the neighborhood of these fields where the summer villages of Nutria, Pescado, and Ojo Caliente are maintained. Mr. Frank H. Cushing has described the old Zuñi method of agriculture. A man without land chose a piece of ground where a gulch opened into a valley or on to the margin of the plain. Across this he made an earthen dam which retained the water and mud brought down during heavy rains. Since the gulch was at ordinary times a dry one, the water did not stand for any length of time but enough of it sank into the ground to supply what moisture was needed for a crop of corn.

Quite contrary to the usual custom among the North American Indians, the men till the fields and do the

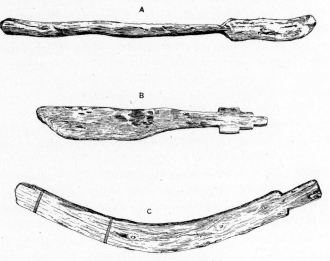

Hoes and Throwing Stick

greater part of the work connected with raising and harvesting the crops. This is probably because in the Southwest agriculture is the chief means of securing food while in other regions it is of less importance than hunting and fishing to which the men principally devote themselves. The only primitive implements used in tilling the soil appear to have been the planting stick and a knife-like wooden paddle which served as a hoe or shovel. Castañeda tells us the ground was not broken before planting the seed. He, of course, greatly exaggerated the productiveness of the soil when he said that one crop was sufficient for seven years. He mentions large quantities of corn in Galisteo Valley stored in underground chambers. The Hopi pueblos still maintain at least a full year's supply of corn to guard against crop failure.

After the corn is gathered it is thoroughly dried either by hanging it in long braids or by spreading it in the sun on the roofs of the buildings. It is stored in the back rooms of the lower stories where the braids are hung up and the loose ears piled in tiers. The pumpkins and squash are cut in long strips which are twisted together and hung about the houses together with many strings of red peppers.

The Hopi and Zuñi have many peach orchards, but fruit was not cultivated when the Spaniards first became acquainted with the Southwest. They did make use of piñon nuts which are frequently mentioned. That they used cherries, wild plums, the fruit of the yucca, and of the various cacti and the pods and beans of the mesquite is also probable, although Castañeda says that pine nuts were the only fruits used by them.

*Preparation of Food.* The method of grinding corn has changed but little since it was first described by Castañeda.

They keep the separate houses where they prepare the food for eating and where they grind the meal, very clean. This is a separate room or closet, where they have a trough with three stones fixed in stiff clay. Three women go in here, each one having a stone, with which one of them breaks the corn, the next grinds it, and the third grinds it again. They take off their shoes, do up their hair, shake their clothes, and cover their heads before they enter the door. A man sits at the door playing on a fife while they grind, moving the stones to the music and singing together. They grind a large quantity at one time, because they make all their bread of meal soaked in warm water, like wafers. (Winship, 522.)

The meal boxes are often in one corner of the living rooms of the modern pueblos and the women still sing at their work but without the accompanying flute. Before grinding, the corn is often parched or roasted.

The wafers mentioned probably refer to piki, the paper-thin bread made of cornmeal of various colors which when rolled or folded is easily portable and keeps indefinitely. This bread is now cooked on a piece of sheet iron or as formerly on thin slabs of stone. Tortillas, having the shape and thickness of pancakes, are also popular. The Hopi place pots of mush in holes in the ground which have been heated by a fire and cover them with ashes and hot coals until they are thoroughly cooked. At Zuñi and along the Rio Grande, the Mexican dome-shaped ovens are generally used.

*Hunting.* The eastern Pueblos, those at Taos, Picuris, and Pecos especially, used to make expeditions to the Plains, principally along the Canadian and Arkansas rivers, to hunt buffalo. Such trips could be made safely only by a large number of men and with the greatest precaution against surprise by the Plains tribes. They were under the control of the war chief as were all communal hunts. The communal hunting of antelope, deer, and elk, because of their scarcity, has been discontinued in recent years, but such hunts for rabbits are still maintained. The men, women, and boys surround a large tract of suitable land, drive the rabbits toward the center and then kill them with bows and arrows and with throwing sticks. These clubs resemble in form the Australian boomerang but do not have the particular character which makes one form of that implement return to the thrower. Deer and antelope may have been hunted in a similar manner, but Captain Bourke in 1881 saw corrals of brush near the Hopi mesas into which antelope were driven. Still hunting by individuals was, of course, practised. Mr. Cushing tells in detail how fetishes were used in such hunts.

Fish are taken for food in the Rio Grande region where there seems to be no taboo against their use. The Zuñi share with their nomadic neighbors, the Navajo and Apache, a dread of anything living in the water. One of the most interesting phases of Southwestern life was the relation existing between the sedentary and nomadic peoples. We are told by the Coronado writers and by Espejo that the nomadic peoples of the Plains and of the mountains of the Southwest brought the meat and the hides of .buffalo and deer to the pueblos and exchanged them for corn and for mantles of cotton. This exchange of products allowed one people to concentrate upon agriculture and the other upon hunting, yet each to have both corn and meat for food, and cotton cloth and dressed skins for clothing.

## DRESS

The dress of the sedentary Indians of the Southwest changed but little from the time it was first described in the sixteenth century until the American occupation and railroads brought other styles and cheaper materials.

In the northeast, at Taos, Picuris, and Pecos, skins were almost, if not quite exclusively worn. The men were described as wearing small shirts with fringes and robes of buffalo skin decorated with painted designs. The women's clothing of these particular pueblos is not mentioned at an early date but even in modern times the long deerskin dresses of the Plains type are occasionally seen at Taos. The dress of the men at this pueblo is hardly distinguishable from that worn by the Indians of the Plains; long leggings, of fringed deerskin, or of red or blue flannel, are still generally worn. The breechcloth of similar flannel is wide and long, hanging nearly to the ground. Deerskin shirts, which are less common, are of the usual Plains type.

Hopi Robe

For all the other pueblos, the sixteenth century dress of the men was an apron or kilt. These were of cotton and are described as resembling napkins of that period but having tassels at each corner. Kilts which are probably similar to these are still worn as ceremonial garments. At the present time a short, narrow breechcloth of white cotton, falling only a few inches from the belt before and behind, is the only essential garment for men at hard work or engaged in ceremonies.

In addition some sort of robe is worn, in winter for added warmth and at other times to complete the costume on ceremonious occasions. In Coronado's time the following were enumerated as the materials employed for these robes: cotton cloth, woven rabbitskins, dressed skins, including that of the buffalo, and turkey feathers attached to a net. Large flocks of turkeys used to be kept chiefly, if not solely, to supply feathers for these garments. Feathered garments have not been in use for many years and woven rabbitskins are rarely employed. The weaving of cotton and wool is still practised by the Zuñi and Hopi, but the woolen blankets of the Navajo and the gayly colored fabrics of the traders have largely displaced them.

The costume of the older men consists of white cotton trousers coming some inches below the knee, but split on the outer side and a cotton shirt falling over the trousers, girded with a cotton belt.

The woman's dress as first described, consisted of a single garment, of yucca fiber at Zuñi, but of cotton elsewhere, which reached from the shoulders to the knees. It was fastened over the right shoulder but open at the left where two tassels hung. A belt was worn at the waist. Later, the material was changed to wool, dyed blue or black and twill woven, but the form remained the same until a few years ago. It is still worn on ceremonial occasions and generally by the older Hopi and Zuñi women. Specimens of the old cotton dresses embroidered in colors with woolen yarn are still in existence. The Museum has a few excellent specimens of these which came from Acoma. The women in the Rio Grande region adopted an undergarment of white cotton which is worn so that the lace border shows below the outer skirt.

The hair of the Zuñi women was described by Castañada as done up above the ears in large whorls. The practice is still maintained in Zuñi ceremonies and by the Hopi maidens who are thus distinguished from the matrons, who wear their hair in two braids. Both men and women, except at Taos and Picuris, wear the front

Woman's Dress.   Acoma

hair banged above the eyes and the side locks cut square, even with the mouth. On the Rio Grande, the men frequently tie their hair with yarn, in two folded clubs, while the Zuñi men make one club of the long hair. At Taos the braids are wrapped with fur or flannel as is the custom of the Plains Indians. The hair of both men and women is frequently washed with yucca root suds.

The moccasins of both men and women have hard soles, a fact emphasized by Castañeda as new and important, who adds that buskins reaching the knee were worn in winter. These are still found in the Rio Grande villages but more generally the women's moccasins are now provided with a long strip of deerskin which is wrapped many times around the lower leg. They are whitened with white earth. Under these leggings are worn footless stockings knit of black or blue woolen yarn.

The ornaments of turquoise and sea shells worn in the ears and about the neck in earlier times were later supplemented by silver beads of native manufacture. The earrings of inlaid turquoise mosaic mentioned by the early Spanish writers are still worn by the Hopi.

The native cotton originally employed in clothing was largely cultivated by the Hopi and to some extent on the Rio Grande below Cochiti in Coronado's time. Very little cotton is now grown. Sheep and wool were introduced at an early date, for we know there were large flocks at the time of the rebellion.

## Industrial Arts

*Pottery.* The household vessels of the modern Pueblo peoples are mostly of clay. These are used for transporting and storing water and for the storage, cooking, and serving of food. The clay is tempered with pottery fragments finely ground. When sufficiently softened with water, a lump of this tempered clay is hollowed to form the nucleus of the bottom of the vessel. To this, round after round of clay, rolled into a slender cylinder, is applied and made to adhere by pressure. The interior and exterior surfaces are modeled with the hand and afterward smoothed with a piece of gourd shell.  Water must constantly be applied to keep the clay in workable condition.  When the vessel has been built in this manner to the desired size and shape, it is allowed to dry thoroughly in the sun.  It is

Santa Clara Woman firing Pottery
(Copyrighted by Fred Harvey)

prepared for ornamentation by polishing it with a pebble and giving it a thin slip of fine clay after which it is repolished.  The designs are then painted on by means of a brush of yucca fiber or a sharpened stick.

San Ildefonso Pottery

The vessels are fired by placing several of them bottom side up on small stones and covering them with dry sheep manure which is used for fuel. This maintains a uniform and continuous heat until they are properly burned.  If the smoke is confined by adding a supply of fresh fine material at the right time, the carbon of the smoke unites with the paint and produced the black ware characteristic of Santa Clara.

This uniformly black ware gains in graceful form what it loses in gay colors.  At San Juan a peculiar form is a pot, red above and undecorated below.  The red applied as a slip is also sometimes used as a background on which designs in other colors are painted. The more common background, however, is the cream color of the uncolored clay to which rarely a little red is added, producing pink.  The designs are painted on in black, obtained from the juice of the bee weed, and in red and yellow derived from ocher.

These designs are partly geometrical and purely decorative; partly representations of mountains, clouds, and rainbows, so highly conventionalized as often to appear purely geometrical; and partly realistic representations of flowers and animals.  Among the latter are most frequently found those which are of economic value, or of ceremonial importance, such as the sunflower, the cotton plant, the parrot, and the turkey. The larger animals like the antelope, frequently seen on Zuñi water jars, have the positions of certain internal organs indicated.

The background of the Hopi pottery has a characteristic yellow tone.  The upper portion of the bowls is often drawn in sharply making the top nearly flat.  The designs, which are of the same general sort found in Rio Grande pottery, are executed in a peculiar style. In recent years both the shapes and the decorations have been considerably modified to meet commercial demands.  This is especially to be noted in the more frequent use of symbols which belong more properly to ceremonial objects.

*Basketry.* Baskets of plaited yucca leaves attached to a heavy wooden rim, quite similar to those found in the prehistoric ruins, are still made by the Zuñi and Hopi. Rude carrying baskets and cradles with a basketry band for the protection of the head are in general use. The Hopi make decorated, nearly flat trays, but

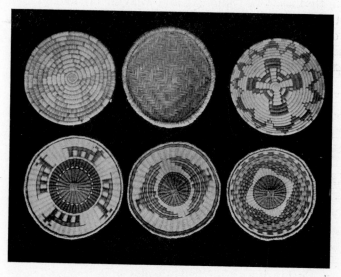

Hopi Baskets

those of Oraibi are strikingly different from those at the middle mesa. The latter use the sewing method and employ very thick foundation coils. The Oraibi make use of wicker work with the foundation material radiating from the center. These flat baskets are used in ceremonies, certain features of which the decorations often symbolize.

*Weaving.* Recently, weaving, which flourished in earlier centuries, has declined; at first because of the

large output of the neighboring Navajo and later because of the introduction of European goods.  The
garments needed in the ceremonies are still made by the
Hopi and every bridegroom must weave or have woven
a trousseau for his bride.  The implements and processes
are those employed by the Navajo and will be described
in that section.  Spinning and weaving are looked upon
by the Hopi as the work of the men and are generally
done by them in the kivas.

Hopi Pottery

## DECORATIVE ART

Decorative art is chiefly displayed in freehand painting on the surface of pottery vessels.  The geometrical
patterns are well devised and well executed.  Both
flowers and animals are reproduced with no attempt at
perspective, real talent or genius in drawing never being
displayed.  Apparently the older art gave way under
European influences to new forms which, for some
reason, have not reached the perfection of the old seen
in the black and white ware from the Tularosa ruins and
the excellently colored vessels from the Little Colorado.
Since we know certain of the villages in the latter
region were deserted at an early date, we are justified in

concluding that this art reached its climax before the beginning of the historic period.

Symbolic art, while found upon pottery, is particularly developed in ceremonial painting and carving. Symbols in which semicircles stand for clouds, zigzag arrows for lightning, and vertical lines for rain are common, and many other conventions are employed. The prayer bowls and the wooden headdresses worn in dances often have their tops fashioned in terraced rectangles which, in the east, represent both mesas and mountain peaks and stand in general for the earth, but are clouds to the Zuñi and sun ladders to the Hopi. In the dry or sand paintings, described in another section, excellent flat representations of animals are reproduced.

It is difficult in a sentence or a paragraph to give the reader an adequate conception of the extent to which color and number enter into the myths, songs, prayers, and ceremonial observations. All important things are repeated for each of the cardinal points with changing color and symbolism. The movements in ceremonies are from the north to the west or counter clockwise. The colors are yellow for the north; blue for the west; red for the south; white for the east; all colors, or mixed, for the zenith; and black for below. These conceptions of color and number while put to a ceremonial use are almost certainly of the same aesthetic origin which has produced symmetry, repetition, and rhythm in geometrical decoration.

## SOCIAL ORGANIZATION

It is now recognized that with people everywhere, as well as with ourselves, the biological family consisting of the father and mother with their children is the

important unit in social organization. When these
children marry they may, without regard to sex, remain
in the parental home with their spouses and children, or
they may leave, founding new homes. Among some
peoples the prevailing practice is for the sons only to
remain with or near their father's home, while the
daughters go with their husbands to other localities.
The reverse frequently happens, that daughters remain and the sons-in-law are joined to the growing
family. Among the Hopi and Zuñi, at least, this latter
practice prevails. The young man, when accepted,
comes to live with his wife's family. Later, his wife
secures or builds for herself a new house or a set of
rooms which usually adjoins her mother's. This house
is her property and a dissatisfied husband in the case
of a separation leaves his wife in possession of the
family home and returns to the house of his mother
or a sister.

Descent is chiefly reckoned through the mother and
the counting of relationship in the female line is maintained from generation to generation indefinitely. All
the members of such a group consider themselves
relatives of a kind and degree appropriate to the ages
and generations of the particular individuals. These
groups of people who consider themselves related
through their mothers are generally referred to as clans.

Not only does a form of relationship prevail throughout such groups, with appropriate terms of relationship,
but this kinship is considered to be of such a degree
that marriage between two members of the same clan
cannot be considered. Technically the clans are exogamous, or in other words they are "incest groups."
It would be perhaps impossible for such large groups to
exist and function without a name by which they can
be distinguished or designated. Notwithstanding that

the villages are numerous and widely scattered, and that four distinct languages are spoken in them, the names associated with these clans are in meaning the same or at least similar. According to Professor Kroeber the names and associates are as follows:—

1. *a,* Rattlesnake; *b,* Panther
2. *a,* Deer; *b,* Antelope
3. *a,* Squash; *b,* Crane
4. *a,* Cloud; *b,* Corn
5. *a,* Lizard; *b,* Earth
6. *a,* Rabbit; *b,* Tobacco
7. *a,* Tansy Mustard; *b,* Chaparral Cock
8. Kachina: *a,* Raven; *b,* Macaw; *c,* Pine; *d,* Cottonwood
9. *a,* Firewood; *b,* Coyote
10. *a,* Arrow; *b,* Sun; *c,* Eagle; *d,* Turkey
11. *a,* Badger; *b,* Bear
12. *a,* Turquoise; *b,* Shell Coral

While these precise designations do not occur in every instance they are clearly representative of the general meaning of the clan names.

It will be noticed that these clans are grouped, usually in pairs. This grouping is more than merely formal since a definite degree of relationship is felt to bind together the members of one of the pair to the members of the other. In some instances this is so strong that the pair have become one exogamous group and no intermarriage takes place. This is true among the Hopi of the Kachina and Parrot clans. In the villages on the Rio Grande the clans are grouped into two divisions or moieties known as the winter people and the summer people. This separation of the people and the year into two divisions plays a prominent part in social games, in political matters, and in the ceremonies.

These clans seem to serve two functions in the community. In the first place they are similar to families, but they are larger groups with more slender ties binding them together, and only one parent, in this case the mother, is considered in reckoning the relationship. The relationship tie, however, is sufficient to carry the right of special hospitality. Secondly, certain political and religious duties devolve upon clans as such or upon individuals because of their clan membership.

The clans have no definite organization or officers, nor do they own houses or other secular property. Each clan owns a fetish which is kept in a certain house and cared for by the householder. It results that these particular houses and persons become centers of interest for the respective clans. Among the Hopi certain eagle nests are the property of particular clans. In the large villages, such as Zuñi and Oraibi, a localization of clans in the community structure results from the natural spread of the family in which the women own the houses and women who are related by blood choose to live side by side.

Nothing is known concerning the origin of these clans. There are similar social divisions elsewhere in North America and other parts of the world. They are best considered as purely social phenomena either as larger family groups or as subdivisions of the political or ethnic units. It is certain that the clans in the Southwest could not have resulted in the manner related in the myths of the Hopi, since the wide distribution of these clans in the Southwest with names of common meaning makes such an origin next to impossible.

## Social Customs

The Hopi baby is first washed and dressed by its paternal grandmother or by one of her sisters. On the day of its birth, she makes four marks with cornmeal on the four walls of the room. She erases one of these on the fifth, tenth, fifteenth, and twentieth day of the child's life. On each of these days the baby and its mother have their heads washed with yucca suds. On the twentieth day, which marks the end of the lying-in period, the grandmother comes early, bathes the baby, and puts some cornmeal to its lips. She utters a prayer in which she requests that the child shall reach old age and in this prayer gives it a name. A few of the women members of the father's clan come in one at a time, bathe the baby, and give it additional names. After the names have been given, the paternal grandmother goes with the mother and the child to the eastern edge of the mesa, starting so as to arrive there about sunrise. Two ears of white corn which have been lying near the child during the twenty days are carried with them. The grandmother touches these ears of corn to the baby's breast and waves them toward the east. She also strews cornmeal toward the sun, placing a little on the child's mouth; meanwhile, she prays, uttering in the course of her prayer the various names which have been given to the child. The mother goes through a similar ceremony and recites a similar prayer.

The names given relate in some way to the clan of the one who bestows them. Of the various names given the child, one, because it strikes the fancy of the family, becomes the child's name which is retained until the individual is initiated into some ceremony, usually between the ages of fifteen and eighteen. At that time, a new name, which is usually retained throughout the individual's life, is given by the man or woman who is sponsor for the novice.

At the present time at least, the Hopi young people arrange their own marriages. When their minds are thoroughly made up, and the young man has acquired some property, the parents are informed of the matter. Marriages usually take place in the fall or winter. The first step is for the mother of the girl to accompany her to the young man's house with a tray of white corn-meal. She gives this to the young man's mother and returns to her home. The girl remains and grinds corn for three days. In the morning of the fourth day, the relatives of the couple assemble at the bridegroom's house. The two future mothers-in-law prepare two large bowls of yucca suds. With one of these the mother of the girl washes the boy's head and the boy's mother does the same for the girl. The other female relatives present assist in rinsing the suds from the hair.

When the washing is finished, the bridal pair take a pinch of cornmeal and walk silently to the eastern side of the mesa. They breathe upon the cornmeal, throw it toward the rising sun, and utter a short prayer. Upon their return to the young man's house, the marriage itself is considered complete, although the ceremony is not. The girl assists her mother-in-law in preparing a breakfast which is eaten by the members of both families. After the meal, the father of the young man runs out of the house and distributes bolls of cotton to the friends and relatives who are expected to separate the seeds from the cotton.

A few days later, the crier announces that the spinning of the cotton is to take place. The men relatives and friends gather in their kivas and spend the day in carding and spinning cotton which they bring in the evening to the bridegroom's house where they partake of a feast. From the cotton yarn prepared in this way, the father of the bridegroom, assisted by the other men of the family, weaves two large white robes and a white fringed girdle. A pair of moccasins provided with long deerskin strips is also made. The blanket and the moccasins are coated with white earth. When the outfit has been completed, which usually takes six or seven weeks, the bride is dressed by her mother-in-law in the moccasins and one of the robes. She takes the other robe, wrapped in a reed mat, in her hands and goes to her mother's house, where her husband also appears during the day. They live with the girl's people for some months until a new home is prepared.

The preparation of clothing for the bride by the bridegroom or men of his family is evidently an old custom, for Castañeda mentions it as being the practice in his day on the Rio Grande. Villagran, who in 1610 wrote a long poem on the conquest and settlement of New Mexico, describes a wedding during which the robes of the pair were tied together. A similar rite is still maintained at Santo Domingo.

Among the Zuñi the bride receives a present from the bridegroom and frequently carries presents to her mother-in-law during a period extending over a year, or until her first child is born. The bridegroom's first visits to the home of his new wife are clandestine and following his visits the bride herself avoids her family, apparently from motives of shame. The man soon takes up his regular abode at the home of his wife and works for the benefit of her family. While the Zuñi relations are strictly monogamous the marriage tie is fairly brittle. It is always the husband who leaves, since the house is the woman's permanent home.

Among the Rio Grande villages the Catholic marriage ceremony is usually conducted.

When an adult dies among the Hopi, the nearest relatives by blood wash the head, tie a feather offering

to the hair so that it will hang over the forehead, wrap
the body in a good robe, and carry it to one of the grave-
yards which are on or near the mesas. Within a few
hours after death, the body is buried in a sitting position
so that it faces the east. The third night, a bowl containing some food, a prayer-stick offering, and a feather
and string offering are carried to the grave. The string
is placed so that it points from the grave toward the
west. The next morning, the fourth, the soul is supposed to rise from the grave, and proceed in the direction indicated by the string where it enters the "skeleton
house." This is believed to be situated somewhere near
the canyon of the Colorado.

The bodies of children who have not yet been initiated into some society are not buried in the ground
but are placed in a crevice of the rock somewhere in
the side of the mesas and covered with stones. The
string offering in this case is not placed pointing toward
the west, but toward the house where the family lives.
The spirit of the child is believed to return to the house
and to be reborn in the body of the next child, or to
linger about the house until the mother dies, when it
accompanies her to the world of the departed.

Among the Zuñi it is the relatives of the father of the
household who carry out the duties connected with death
and burial. The bodies are placed in the churchyard,
the men on the south side and the women on the north
side with the head to the east, which is also the position
of burial among the Keresans. The souls are supposed
to go in four days' time to the sacred lake 65 miles
southwest of Zuñi. After this interval, a purification
of the family and their belongings takes place. The
personal property of the deceased, which is not required
for the proper dressing of the corpse, is burned or buried
apart on the river bank.

## POLITICAL ORGANIZATION

The political government of each Rio Grande pueblo is in the hands of a governor, council, and a war chief. The governor, chosen annually by a formal election, is in reality named by the cacique, a permanent officer whose duties are chiefly religious. There is usually also a lieutenant governor chosen in the same way. The war chief too is appointed annually and confirmed by the council.

This council, which is the legislative body, is permanent in some pueblos, but elected annually in others. It is believed by some to be a survival of an earlier council in which each of the clans was represented by its head.

The governor is the representative of the village in its dealings with other villages and with the general public and is its nominal head. The war chief directs all communal work such as that on the irrigation ditches and the communal hunt. In earlier times he led the war expeditions and had charge of the defense of the pueblo. He is the executive officer of the council and carries out its decrees. These frequently have involved the death of persons suspected of witchcraft.

The Hopi pueblos each have a village chief, a crier chief, and a war chief who hold their positions for life.

The older methods of defensive warfare are well illustrated in the accounts of conflicts between the Spaniards and certain Pueblos in the sixteenth century. At Zuñi the men withdrew to the house tops and pulled up the ladders. When the Spaniards advanced within reach, arrows were discharged and stones were thrown down. The women, children, and old men had been sent to other villages or to Thunder Mountain. Similar methods were resorted to at Tiguex, where a besieged pueblo held out for many months because occasional falls of snow furnished a fresh supply of water. Pecos, which had a wall and a spring inside, was said by Castañeda to have resisted successfully the attacks of Plains Indians.

The weapons used were bows and arrows, a stone-headed club, and a stick half a yard long, set with flints, which Espejo says would split a man asunder. For the protection of the warriors, rawhide shields, leather jackets, and head pieces of leather are mentioned.

## Religious Practices

The religious activities of the sedentary people of the Southwest are so many and so intricate that it is difficult to describe or discuss them, especially in so limited a space. There are some common elements, however, which are worthy of notice. The ceremonies often take the form of dramas in which the movements and activities of supernatural beings and animals are imitated. The actors wear masks, paint their bodies, and conduct themselves according to the supposed appearance and character of the divinity or animal represented. The divinities are also represented by larger stone images rudely shaped and by smaller ones which are better executed in stone or wood.

There are permanent shrines usually near the villages, often walled in on three sides and sometimes sheltering an image or a peculiarly shaped stone. Temporary altars are made during the ceremonies by setting up a line of wooden slabs carved or painted with religious symbols before which dry paintings are placed. These dry paintings are made by sprinkling sand of various colors so as to form symbols and pictures of the gods.

Small sticks, singly or in pairs, are painted and often have faces indicated on them. Feathers and a corn-husk containing cornmeal and honey are usually attached to them. They are placed at the shrines and springs for the deities. Cornmeal and pollen are strewed and thrown toward the sun. Cornmeal is also frequently used to mark ceremonial trails and to define the limits of sacred places. Races generally occur during the ceremonies but their significance is not clear. Bathing the head and the use of emetics are resorted to as methods of purification.

In general it may be said that Southwestern ceremonials chiefly employ dramatic and graphic art to accomplish their purposes, which appear to be the influencing of invisible supernatural powers and through them the natural forces. The greater number of the ceremonies are intended to bring rain and to aid in fertilizing the crops.

## Rio Grande Ceremonies

It is only from Bandelier's short account of his observations among the Pueblos of the Rio Grande published many years ago, the work of Mrs. Stevenson among the Sia, and a published paper on Cochiti by Father Noël Dumarest, that we are able to get a view at all comprehensive of the religious organization of the Rio Grande region.

At the head of the political and religious systems is the cacique, as he is ordinarily called. The office, which is held for life, requires years of preparatory training and study and its duties are arduous. The cacique is expected to devote himself to a life of fasting and prayer. His fasts vary from slight temporary self-denials to absolute abstinence of four days' duration, according to the seriousness of the people's need. He is the mouthpiece of the divinities whom he is called upon by the tribe or by individuals to consult. Because he is believed to speak by divine authority his influence is very great. He names his successor and nominates the civil officers of the village. He is not supposed, however, to enter into petty quarrels nor to take part in minor discussions in the council. That he may be free to devote himself to such a life his wants are provided for by his people who supply him with wood and cultivate a field for his benefit. He has one or two assistants from whom his successor is chosen.

There are many societies more or less secret, which have the knowledge of certain prayers, songs, and rites,

Hopi Prayer Offerings

which they are expected to use for the public benefit. The most important is a group of societies which are especially devoted to ceremonies leading to success in war. Among the Sia these societies are those of the Panther, Bear, and Knife. Their leader, the war priest, ranks next to the cacique in religious importance. He holds his office for life and nominates his successor. His duties include the active control of the more important religious ceremonies. The hunters in earlier days were also important since they had the fetishes and the ceremonies by the aid of which game could be taken. The panther was their patron for he was looked upon as the most successful hunter. The head priest of the hunters was also a most important person. Finally, the many societies (among the Sia, the Snake, Spider, Ant, etc.) which have the power of healing diseases and producing rain have, according to Bandelier, one head shaman, whose office gives him great power, particularly in the discovery and punishment of witches.

Then there are two societies or classes of priests, the cuirana, or winter priests, and the koshare, the summer priests, to use the Keresan terms. The former, by their activities, cause the seeds to germinate, while the latter bring the crops, and all animal and human life as well, to maturity. It is the koshare who act as clowns on all public religious occasions. Each of these societies has a leader who, with the cacique and the head priest of the warriors, hunters, and healers, constitute a most important sacerdotal group.

All male adults are expected at some time to participate in the kachina dances. Masks and headdresses are worn to represent a special class of supernatural beings, the greater number of whom at least are the souls of the dead. They are the senders of the rain and therefore the bringers of good fortune and happiness. Boys go through an initiation which consists of a beating and then one of the dancers unmasks that the child may see that the gods are not present in person as he has formerly supposed. The women in theory are never supposed to know that the masked dancers are not in reality the gods they appear to be.

*Sia Rain Ceremony.* Mrs. Stevenson, who witnessed several of the ceremonies of the Sia, has given a full description of the rain ceremony of the snake order. Notched and colored prayer-sticks were prepared for offering. An altar with a dry painting representing clouds by terraced semicircles was made. On it were placed several fetishes and a clan or society emblem called *yaya* which is a perfectly kerneled ear of corn entirely covered with feathers.

The ceremony proper begins with the strewing of a line of cornmeal from the altar to the door over which as a road the spirits of the gods are supposed to travel and temporarily enter the fetishes. There is much singing, dancing, and praying, mostly by individuals rather than in concert. In a bowl of water to which ground yucca roots have been added, a suds is made which represents clouds. Pollen is sprinkled into this bowl and the foam is scattered over the altar.

By means of songs and prayers the gods who dwell in six sacred springs are invoked that they may incite the cloud people to action. Near each of these springs there is supposed to be a hollow tree through which the cloud people carry the water up to the clouds. These clouds are but huge masks behind which the cloud people climb and from which they sprinkle the earth. The thunders are also invoked. They are thought to be beings with tails and wings of obsidian which clash and make the noise and incite the cloud beings to greater activity.

When the ceremony is finished the sand painting is obliterated and the prayer-sticks carried to a near-by shrine where they are left for the deities. The notches upon these sticks and the painted designs are supposed to convey the message, the attached feathers being given in payment for the favor besought.

*Festivals.* The public ceremonies of the Rio Grande pueblos have taken on the names and some elements of Catholic festivals. They occur on fixed dates which are also the days sacred to their patron saints. There are probably always preliminary activities which are in part rehearsals, held secretly in the kivas, during which, however, prayers are recited and acts of worship performed. The last day is devoted to a public spectacle largely attended by visiting Indians, Mexicans, and others.

Clowns Climbing Pole.   Taos

The ceremony at Taos occurs on September 30th. The image of the saint is brought from the church and placed in an elevated booth overlooking the plaza in which the ceremonies take place. A tall pole erected for the purpose has a great variety of vegetable products, cooked and in their natural state, fastened to its top, where is also suspended the carcass of a sheep which has in recent years replaced that of a deer. The forenoon is devoted to races in which young men from the two large houses compete in relays. The victory is a community and not individual one. The winners are pelted with food by the losers. In the afternoon the clowns appear, men grotesquely dressed and painted, who act as offensively as possible. They take the lunch baskets from women and empty them, tear the clothing from a man, or throw him fully clad into the stream, and enter any house they choose. Finally, they approach the pole as if tracking an animal, attempt to shoot toy arrows to the top, tug at its base as if trying to uproot a tree, and at last make attempts to climb it which succeed for one of their number who secures the food for his fellows. As a whole the ceremony is evidently intended as a consecration of the harvest and an expression of thanksgiving for it.

## Zuñi Ceremonies

At the head of the Zuñi community is a priesthood presided over by the priest of the north who is foremost among the Zuñi in both religious and political activities. The priest representing "the above" is known as the pekwin, the deputy of the sun, and the representative of "the below" is the head bow priest, corresponding to the war priest of the Rio Grande villages. These priests hold office for life. They directly supervise the ceremonial life of the Zuñi and appoint the governor and lieutenant governor with their deputies who hold office from year to year. Each head priest has associated with him assistants who in time may succeed to the head priesthood itself. Mainly it is the duty of this priesthood to fast, to pray, and in other ways to induce rain, insuring the success of the crops and thereby the general happiness of the people.

At death they are succeeded by one of the secondary priests associated with them, usually a relative, brother or son. Because the office does at times pass to a son the position does not belong to a definite clan. The pekwin, however, is an exception since he is chosen from the Dogwood clan by the heads of the fraternities. He is the more active of the priests and controls the ceremonies. He determines the ceremonial calendar by observing the place of the rising and setting of the sun, and proclaims accordingly the time when the ceremonies shall be held.

The priests of the bow have a representative in each fraternity, but together they constitute a priesthood with an elder and younger head priest. These two are the representatives of the war gods. To be eligible as a bow priest the candidate must have taken an enemy's scalp. These war priests are connected with the thunder and are therefore directly concerned with weather control.

In his boyhood every Zuñi man has been initiated into an order or fraternity. At this initiation the boy has as a sponsor the husband of the woman who was present at his birth. The boy becomes associated with the one of the six groups, into which all Zuñi men are divided, to which this sponsor belongs. Each of these groups is associated with a kiva or assembly room of a somewhat sacred character. These organized groups of the Zuñi, directed and presided over by the priesthood, perform the ceremonies and carry on the religious activities of the village.

There are also twelve fraternities concerned chiefly with the curing of disease. Their membership is recruited from those who have been treated for some ailment. Each fraternity has four directing officers one of whom is a bow priest. These fraternities assist in the ceremonies, particularly in supplying the chorus and the leader of the dancers. Members of one of the fraternities, the newekwe, perform as clowns in a manner similar to the koshare or "delight makers" of the Rio Grande villages. Similar in their activities to this fraternity are the koyemshi, but instead of being life-long members of a fraternity or priesthood, they are chosen annually. Their leader is appointed by the

Deer Dance.   Nambe

head rain priest and selects nine others, members of his own fraternity.

The Zuñi year is well filled with public ceremonies the main feature of which is a procession of masked dancers accompanied by a choir of singers and by the antics of the priest clowns. The most impressive of the ceremonies is shalako, which occurs in December. Some phases of this ceremony suggest a European and Catholic origin, while others indicate Navajo influence.

## HOPI CEREMONIES

Among the Hopi two types of ceremonies are held at separate seasons of the year. The kachina ceremonies begin with the winter solstice and terminate in midsummer when a farewell ceremony called the Niman kachina is held. Shortly after, the second series is opened with either the snake dance or the flute ceremony and others follow until November when the new

Hopi Kachina Dolls

fire ceremony completes them. Kachinas are supernatural beings, who during the period when their dances are held, are believed to visit the Hopi. When this season is over, they withdraw to their homes in San Francisco Peaks and elsewhere. They are represented in the dances by men masked and painted to correspond to the traditional conception of the appearance of each kachina. Small wooden images, carved, painted, and decorated with feathers are also used to represent them. Following the Niman kachina these dolls are given to the children as toys.

Ceremonies in which the kachinas appear are of two kinds. The full ceremonies, which are the first held, have, in addition to the public performances, several days devoted to secret rites in the kivas, where altars are made. The abbreviated kachinas, which come late

Snake and Antelope Priests
(Photo by Howard McCormick)

in the spring, have only the dances in the plazas. In these dances, the men who represent the kachinas wear, in addition to the masks, embroidered kilts and sashes. They carry gourd rattles in their hands and have tortoise shell rattles tied to their knees. They move forward slowly in a procession, with mincing steps timed by the rattles, or dance in stationary lines frequently reversing the direction by the wheeling about of the individuals. The priests in charge of the ceremonies and others sprinkle cornmeal on them and pray to them as if they were the real kachina beings. These occasions are enlivened by the pranks of clowns somewhat similar to those of the Rio Grande villages.

The ceremonies of the second series are distinguished from the kachina ceremonies by the absence of masked men and clowns. They are generally spoken of as nine-day ceremonies, although the Hopi themselves

Snake Priests dancing with Snake
(Photo by Howard McCormick)

consider that they last from the day of the formal announcement until their completion sixteen days after. All have certain features in common. Altars are made, prayer-sticks are prepared and offered at various shrines, and there is much praying and singing in the kivas. During the kiva ceremonies, the participants smoke in turn, addressing each other with terms of relationship as the pipe or cigarette is passed. On the last two days of the ceremony there are usually foot races and public performances.

*The Snake Dance.* The most widely known of these ceremonies is the snake dance which is held every second year in all the Hopi pueblos except Hano and Sichumovi. The dances of Walpi and Hotavila are those which attract the largest number of visitors. The ceremony is given jointly by the antelope and snake fraternities. The former is chiefly concerned with the rites in the kiva, while the latter, originally a warrior society, gathers and handles the snakes.

To secure the snakes the snake priests go out in pairs provided with digging-sticks, with snake whips of feathers, and with bags of buckskin or canvas. The first day they go to the north, the second to the west, the third to the south, and the fourth to the east, for this is the ceremonial circuit of the Hopi. If a sufficiently large number is not secured during the four days, snakes are sought in any place and at any time until enough are found. Those used are chiefly rattlesnakes, but bull-snakes and others are also employed. The snakes are usually found by following their trails in the dust. If a snake is uncoiled a little cornmeal is thrown toward it; it is seized by the neck, stroked gently, and placed in a bag. Should the snake coil, a prayer is said and tobacco smoke blown toward it until it uncoils. If the trail of the snake leads to a hole it is dug out with a digging-stick. The snakes gathered are confined in pottery vessels in the kiva until they are wanted for the ceremony.

Both the snake and the antelope priests make altars in their kivas. The snake altar is set up by the Hopi of the third mesa on the evening of the first day. The head priest brings into the kiva two wooden images of great apparent antiquity. The larger represents Pookong, the elder of the war god twins; the smaller may be intended for his brother, or for some other divinity. Near these are placed small images of the panther, the fetish of the warriors and hunters. If a candidate is to be initiated, a sand painting is also made. This has a picture of a panther in the center, a snake on each of the four sides and a frame of four colored bands. Although each band extends entirely around the painting, the outer yellow band represents the north; the second, the green one, the west; the third, red, the south; and the inner white one, the east. These are the colors which the Hopi always associate with the world quarters.

The antelope altar is made in another kiva on the fifth day of the ceremony. The painting consists of a number of semicircular cloud terraces, with a similar border of colored bands. On two sides are rows of sticks, some of them curved, which represent the deceased members of the order. At the back of the altar are the fetishes and the tiponi, the society symbol, kept by the head of the order as a badge of his office. Around this altar a most important rite is held. One of the priests and a woman relative of some member are especially dressed and impersonate antelope man and antelope maiden. The snake priests enter bringing a snake which the antelope man holds during the ceremony. The priests smoke, blowing the smoke toward the altar; clouds of tobacco smoke are also blown from a cloud blower; and a priest appointed for the purpose sprinkles a specially prepared liquid upward and over the altar. Many prayers are uttered and eight songs are sung. This ceremony is repeated each morning after the fifth, throughout the ceremony. A messenger is sent out each afternoon with prayer offerings to be placed on the various shrines. The first day he visits the most distant ones making a circuit of many miles; on the three remaining days the distances are decreased. On the afternoon of the seventh day water is brought by a messenger from a distant spring. Before the water is taken a prayer-stick is set up and the following prayer is uttered:—

Now, then, this here (prayer offerings) I have brought for you. With this I have come to fetch you. Hence, being arrayed in this, thus rain on our crops! Then will these corn-stalks be growing up by that rain; when they mature, we shall be glad over them. Then these our animals when they eat will also be happy over it. Then all living things will be in good condition. Therefore do we thus go to the trouble of assembling. Hence it must be thus. Therefore have pity on us. Now let us go! We shall all go. There let no one keep any one back. You all follow me. (Voth, 320.)

In the early morning of the two last days of the ceremony, two snake priests dressed as warriors pass four times around each of the kivas and enter them. They carry in their hands bullroarers and lightning frames. The first are sticks fastened to strings which, when rapidly whirled, make a noise like falling rain. The lightning frames consist of a series of crossed sticks so joined that they may be quickly projected to a considerable distance and then rapidly returned. These warriors and the messenger who has brought the water the day before, go down on the plain a mile or two from the village. The messenger first makes cloud symbols, deposits a prayer-stick and utters a prayer at four places some distance apart. When he reaches the fourth place the two warriors advance toward him, swinging their bullroarers and shooting out the lightning frames. When they reach the fourth place of offering, the runners start toward the village. The first one passing the messenger is given the netted gourd containing the water brought from the distant spring. This he must surrender to any one passing him so that the winner arrives with it at the village. As the runners approach the mesa, they are joined, on the eighth morning by antelope priests and on the ninth morning by snake priests. Boys follow them up the mesa trails with freshly cut cornstalks. When the runners have passed, the girls of the village snatch these cornstalks from the boys and carry them to the houses to be used as decorations.

About noon of the ninth day an interesting feature of the ceremony takes place in the snake kiva. A liquid is prepared in a vessel kept for the purpose; the snakes are dipped into it and then placed on some sand to dry in the sun which shines through the hatchway at that hour. At Walpi, however, they are thrown with considerable violence upon the sand painting of the altar.

Public performances in the plaza take place in the afternoon of the eighth and ninth days. The antelope priests first come from their kiva and go in procession four times around the plaza. As they pass in front of a booth which has been provided for the snakes, each man stamps on a plank which has been placed there to represent the place of exit from the lower world. When the fourfold circuit has been completed, they form in a line at either side of the booth. The snake priests then come out and make a similar circuit four times around the plaza and form in a line facing the booth and the antelope priests. Each line is led by its head priest. The antelope priest is also accompanied by a sprinkler who carries a vessel filled with liquid.

On the eighth day, the lines dance for some time facing each other. Then the sprinkler goes to the snake booth, takes a small bundle of vines and corn stalks in his mouth and dances with it as if it were a snake. He is guarded by a snake priest. But on the ninth day after the two lines of priests have made the circuit of the plaza the snake priests go in pairs to the booth. One of each pair is given a snake which he holds in his mouth. His companion follows by his side with a snake whip with which he is prepared to soothe the snake and attract its attention should there be need. In this way they move down the plaza for some yards and then the snake is dropped. Each pair of dancers is followed by a third snake priest who picks up the snakes as they fall and keeps them in his hands. When his hands are full, he passes some of the snakes to the antelope priests who are still in line. The dancers return for additional snakes until the entire number, fifty or more, have been carried in the dance. The head snake priest then makes a large circle of cornmeal and draws six radii which represent the six world directions. Into this circle the snakes are thrown in a heap and the women sprinkle them plentifully with cornmeal. At a given signal the snake priests approach, grab as many snakes as they can hold in each hand, run down the trails to the plain, and release the snakes.

In alternate years the flute ceremony is held in place of the snake dance. This ceremony is given by two orders, the blue and drab flute priests. The final public ceremony takes place at certain springs where songs and prayers are rendered. The rite is characterized by playing on long flutes. An interesting feature of the ceremony is the placing of prayer offerings at the bottom of a deep spring for which purpose a priest enters it.

Following the snake and flute ceremonies are other nine-day ceremonies given by societies of women. During the public performance of one society, the Mamzrauti, the women carry in their hands large wooden slabs on which kachinas, cloud symbols, and ears of

corn are painted. Following this is the Ooqol ceremony. Alternating with these two ceremonies, the
Lalakonti dance is given. During the public dance of
both the Ooqol and the Lalakonti ceremonies, darts
are thrown at netted wheels and basket trays are
waved in the hands of the dancers. These trays are
later given to the spectators.

The Marau Society dancing the Mamzrauti at Mishongnovi
(Photo by Dr. R. H. Lowie)

The last of this series of ceremonies is held in October
or November. All the male fraternities join in its
celebration. The chief feature is the making of a new
fire by means of a firedrill. While this is taking place,
the trails to the village are closed by drawing a line
of cornmeal across them.

The greater number of the Hopi ceremonies are for
the purpose of bringing rain, maintaining the water in

the springs, and increasing the yield of the fields. These ceremonies are given by fraternities of priests whose members are recruited by taking in those who have been cured or benefited by the order. A person who has been bitten by a rattlesnake applies to a member of the snake fraternity for treatment. It is then proper for him to be initiated and become a participant in the ceremonies. The leadership in these orders usually passes to a brother or to a sister's son and remains in the same clan. In Hopi thought these fraternities are associated with the clan to which the leader belongs.

## RELIGIOUS BELIEFS

Of the many religious concepts entertained by the Pueblo people certain ones seem to be common to all. It is generally believed that the ancestors of the present people came up from underground to the surface of the world. The Rio Grande peoples say the place of emergence is to the north near the sources of the river near which they live. The Zuñi point to a certain lake in their own neighborhood; the Hopi conceive the place to be in the canyon of the Colorado. The souls of the dead return through the same opening to the underworld in a journey of four days. These souls of the dead are not confined underground but also visit the mountains and the sky where they appear as clouds. The war gods among the Hopi are dwarfs about whom there are amusing tales, but in the east, on the Rio Grande and at Zuñi, they are important deities. There is some evidence that they are thunder gods. Of the objects of nature the sun seems to hold the first place. Among the Rio Grande villages, however, a mother who still resides at the place of emergence holds a high place among the divinities. That she represents the earth is probable. The winds and the lightning have a place with the clouds mentioned above. The world quarters are also included, but the nature of the concept is vague. Probably persons are supposed to reside in them but certain animals are also associated with the world quarters. Panther is the patron of the hunters and bear of the healers. These animal gods and others are represented by images large and small. There are also the great stone panthers of Old Cochiti and the numerous images and fetishes of the Zuñi.

In addition to the small animal representations used as fetishes there are others, less definite in form and probably symbolic in character. There is evidence that all the villages, except perhaps some of the Tewa pueblos, have a fetish for each clan, for each prominent fraternity, and for the head priest. They are perhaps the most sacred objects possessed by the Pueblo peoples, and about them centers much of the social and religious life. The Zuñi fetishes are sections of reeds together with various sacred objects wrapped in cotton. They are deposited in a jar which is kept in a room of a house which is the center and place of gathering for the particular group. Each Zuñi individual at the time of his initiation into the society of the gods receives an ear of corn covered with feathers. This is his personal fetish; it is carried by him on certain ceremonial occasions; and is buried on the river bank at his death. The Keresans of Laguna and the Hopi have similar wrapped ears of corn which correspond in use to the Zuñi fetishes of reeds mentioned above. One is owned by each head of a fraternity and there is one for each clan which is kept in a house which becomes, as a result, the clan center.

We have then in the Southwest a peculiar jumble of objects which are adored, including natural features, persons, and animals, with the souls of ancestors occupying a prominent place.

# Chapter III

# THE VILLAGE DWELLERS

## The Pima and Papago

CONSIDERATION so far has been given to those natives of the Southwest who live or did live in the community dwellings which are large enough to accommodate several or many families. This very special trait of community building and dwelling distinguishes these people from others in this same region. There are other groups almost equally sedentary who are, however, housed in one-family houses grouped into fairly permanent villages.

The Pima and Papago, as they are designated, are the most important tribes living in villages of one-family houses. To the Spaniards the territory was known as Pimeria and it was divided into Pimeria Alta and Pimeria Baja. The former was occupied by the Pima and Arizona Papago and the latter by the Papago of Sonora. In early Spanish times there were villages on the San Pedro and Santa Cruz rivers occupied by the Sobaipuri who, as far as we know, are distinguishable from the Pima and Papago only on geographical and political grounds. If there were variations in language or culture no record of these differences remains. Missions were established among them in the latter part of the seventeenth and the early part of the eighteenth centuries. One of these was at San Xavier del Bac, a village now occupied by the Papago. The Sobaipuri were forced westward by the Apache who occupied Aravaipa Creek, a tributary of the San Pedro. It is supposed the Sobaipuri remnants joined the Pima and were absorbed by them.

The Pima lived along the Gila River, Arizona, for some thirty miles above the junction of that stream with the Salt River. They were in this locality when first noticed in Spanish writings. The date is difficult to establish, but there can be little doubt that the first definite and direct European influence was that exerted by Father Eusebio Francisco Kino who traveled through this region between the years 1687 and 1710. The first description of the Pima is the account of a visit to their villages on November 21, 1697, by Father Kino, accompanied by Juan Mateo Mange, who wrote the official report of the journey. That European goods and influence had reached the Pima indirectly before this time is probable. They were friendly from their very first meeting with the Spaniards and manifested the same amiability toward the Americans who began to penetrate their country in the second third of the nineteenth century. From the discovery of gold in California until the building of the railroad, their villages were a stopping place for Americans who followed the southern route.

The number of their villages in Spanish and American times has varied between five and ten. It should not be assumed that they would be quite so permanent as the community structures of the Pueblo Indians. In 1902 Professor Frank Russell enumerated eighteen villages. The report of the Commissioner of Indian Affairs for 1923 gives the number of Pima as 5592.

The Maricopa, a Yuman people, are believed to have joined the Pima early in the nineteenth century. They had been moving slowly eastward for some years under the pressure of the Yuma on the Colorado River. The Maricopa numbered only 394 in 1923. They live on the Salt River and have become entirely similar to the Pima except in language and burial customs.

South of the Gila live the Papago. Their villages are situated wherever there is arable land that can be irrigated. They occupy the region south of the Pima for 150 miles or more extending a considerable distance into Sonora, Mexico, and westward quite or nearly to the Gulf of California. The Report of the Commissioner of Indian Affairs for 1923 gives the number of 5672 living in Arizona. The figures for those living in Mexico are not available, but are estimated at about 700. The Papago are not so sedentary as the Pima since in many instances a group maintains a winter village in the mountains where water and forage are more plentiful for their herds, as well as a summer village for the raising of their crops. Ordinarily, the winter village is the more permanent.

## Houses

The Pima dwelling house has the shape of a dome or an inverted bowl, considerably flattened. Its circular groundplan is on the average about 18 feet in diameter. Within this circle four posts are set up at the corners of a rectangle about seven by eight feet. These posts are forked at the top and in the forks are placed beams on which lighter cross pieces rest. This framework forms the support for the outer shell which consists of willow poles set in the ground and drawn in at the top to form the flattened dome. The willow poles are held in place by horizontal pieces tied in place with willow bark. Over this framework is placed a thatch of brush and straw and on top of that a layer of earth 5 to 10 inches deep. There is only one opening, a low doorway through which one must stoop to enter. No special opening is provided for the smoke from the fire, which passes out of the top of the doorway while the fresh cold air comes in at the bottom. The occupants either recline or sit to avoid the smoke which fills the domed ceiling.

Situated near the house is usually a flat-topped shade, a type of structure which is nearly universal in the Southwest. In summer the cooking is done outside and no fire in the house is necessary, but in winter a fire is maintained for warmth. The outdoor cooking fire is provided with a simple windbreak, the simplest and most essential type of domicile.

A Pima Dwelling
(Photo by Mary Lois Kissell)

It is said that in former times each village had a community house similar in structure to the dwellings but oval in groundplan, which in some cases was capable of holding eighty people. No such houses are now standing among the Pima.

The Papago house differs from that of the Pima only in the material and perhaps the size. Instead of cottonwood posts, mesquite is used for the main supports, and ribs of the giant cactus take the place of willow poles. The ceremonial lodges of the Papago are

of the same type as the dwellings but usually larger.
It is presumed that they correspond in use to the
oval council houses of the Pima.

The food of the Pima and the Papago in a general
way is similar to that of the pueblo dwellers. They
live in part upon domesticated animals and plants
and in part upon wild animals and wild vegetable
products. For the Papago at least, the proportion of
wild food is greater than with the Pueblo people.
Before Spanish times the cultivated crops were maize,
squash, beans, and cotton. Wheat seems to have been
introduced at an early date, perhaps even before direct
contact with the Spaniards. It is well adapted to
the soil and climate and has become the most important of the cultivated crops. Considerable quantities
of corn and wheat were furnished to the various expeditions and travelers passing the Pima villages during the
middle of the nineteenth century. A small breed of
fowl was introduced among the Papago and reached
the Pima. They also acquired horses, donkeys,
cattle, sheep, and goats. As far as the environment
would permit, they became Europeanized in the matter
of domesticated animals and crops at least a century
ago. Oxen with wooden plows are used in some cases
for plowing, especially among the Papago. Cattle were
never abundant, for until recently it was the custom to
kill and eat all the cattle at the death of the owner.
They continue, however, the primitive methods of cul-
tivating corn. This is done by turning the water of the
rivers, or impounded storm waters, into a ditch by
means of which the crops are irrigated. The weeds
which grow luxuriantly are removed with a knife-
shaped, wooden implement. The water of the Gila has
ordinarily a great deal of silt held in suspension which is
spread over the valley land by the process of irrigation.

The farms as a result are not only very fertile but they are easily worked, since this deposit is very friable.

Besides using the flesh of the domesticated animals, the Pima and Papago successfully hunted for antelope and deer which were found scattered generally over their habitat. Mountain sheep are still found on the mountains of southern Arizona and northwestern Mexico.

Notwithstanding that much of the country is classed as desert, valuable wild food is secured in large quantities. The most esteemed seems to be the giant cactus or sahuara. The native year begins with the sahuara harvest which is celebrated by one of the important festivals. The fruit is gathered in the early part of July. The ripe fruit is dried and pressed into large cakes consisting of the edible pulp and the small black seeds. The dried pulp is boiled for a long time and ground on a metate before it is eaten. The seeds are separated, ground, and mixed with water to form a gruel. Food in this form, finely ground corn, wheat, or seeds, eaten either dry or mixed with water, is known as piñole in the Southwest. The juice from the fresh sahuara fruit is extracted, boiled, and allowed to ferment. The wine so secured is a main feature of the harvest festival.

The mesquite furnishes food in considerable quantities. The pods are edible. When dry they are easily pulverized, producing a sweet and very agreeable flour. There are various species of cacti which are used for food. The barrel cactus, when crushed, furnishes a large quantity of liquid which is a good substitute for water.

The desert flora, moreover, is fairly independent of seasonal rains.

## CLOTHING

One article of the clothing of the Pima and Papago sets them off from practically all other Indians within the confines of the United States. Sandals clearly belong to the south. They are worn in South and Central America and in Mexico. The Pima and Papago wear in summer a sandal of thick rawhide. The prehistoric peoples of the Southwest wore sandals of woven leaves and fiber, as has been noted above, but their use has been retained by none of the other present-day inhabitants of this region. When going abroad for a considerable distance, moccasins are substituted for sandals which give insufficient protection to the feet in this thorn beset country. Until fairly recently the men during the greater part of the year wore only these sandals and a small cotton breechcloth. In cold weather a deerskin shirt and a cotton blanket or a robe of woven rabbitskins was added. The women, throughout the year, wear a cotton blanket girded around the waist and falling to the knees. In winter all but the recent widows pull the folds of these blankets over their shoulders.

## BASKETRY AND TEXTILES

A variety of textile processes is employed by the Pima and Papago. Plaiting, which, as has been mentioned above, was employed by the prehistoric peoples and is still known to the Pueblo peoples, is used in the manufacture of mats and a certain class of baskets. This plaiting is diagonal and for mats is done with the leaves of a reed. The rectangular covered baskets used to hold trinkets and medicine outfits are made chiefly by the Papago women who employ agave leaves. The greater number of the baskets, however, are sewed on a coiled foundation. In general appearance these

baskets are very similar to those made by the Apache
and other neighboring tribes. The coiled foundation
of the Pima and Papago baskets, however, consists of
a bundle of small strands. The Pima formerly used
the leaves of a rush which grew near the Gila River.

Pima Trays

The Papago, and in recent years the Pima, use the
leaves of a yucca. The sewing material, which is
visible on the basket, is of willow twigs from which the
bark has been removed and the twig itself split and trimmed to a convenient size. The Papago now make many

Pima Storage Basket

baskets for the tourist trade, using for such baskets the white, bleached leaves of a yucca. Their older baskets, however, were of willow, as are those of the Pima. This white material covers the body of the basket and forms the background for the designs, which are in black or dark brown. This dark material is derived from the fruit pods of the martynia or catsclaw.

The designs consist chiefly of narrow strips which zigzag and radiate from the bottom of the basket toward the rim. One noticeable feature of these coiled baskets is that the beginning is of plaited work while similar baskets in other parts of the Southwest are begun by the same coiling method which is used in the main portion of the basket.

The Pima and Papago also make large storage baskets by a coiling method which does not involve the use of a second element to hold the coils together. They are bound together by an interlocking of the twigs which make up the succeeding coils.

One of the important uses to which baskets are put throughout western North America is as a container for small objects which are to be transported on the backs of the women. The Apache have such baskets, which are usually made by twining, not by coiling. The Pima and Papago do not make or use burden-baskets, but have instead a net of twine supported on a frame of poles called *kiaha*. The fiber for the twine is secured from the leaves of the sotol (*Dasylirion wheeleri*) and probably also from the narrow leaved yucca. The net is made by a method of interlocking of stitches, known as lace coiling. The supporting frame consists of sticks fashioned from the ribs of the giant cactus. A hoop of willow holds the mouth of the net open. Twine made of human hair is used to bind this loop to the projecting ends of the frame. This carrying net is not only an object well adapted to its use, but is a part of the woman's costume and therefore decorated as if it were a garment. The younger women are more particular about the ornamental characters of their *kiaha* than are the older women.

The headbands and belts of the Pima and Papago are of the same sort found southward in western Mexico among the Huichol and among the Hopi and the

Pima Plaited Basket

Navajo to the north. They are woven on a special loom one end of which is attached to a tree or post and the other to the waist of the seated weaver. Wool is used in recent years for the warp of these belts, the weft being of cotton.

The early Spanish accounts mention the growing of cotton and the weaving of cloth with which the Pima clothed themselves. Cotton was raised to some extent until the close of the last century. The spindle was a simple shaft with a cross piece near one end to give momentum in whirling. The spinning was generally done by the women. In structure, the loom is similar to that still used by the Pueblo and Navajo Indians. It is interesting to note, however, that the loom was stretched horizontally near the ground instead of being suspended vertically as is the case elsewhere. As far as is known, the products of the looms were simple in character, suitable pieces for folding about the body and for use as blankets. The older men did the weaving.

## SOCIAL ORGANIZATION

It will be recalled that the pueblo-dwelling peoples of the Southwest, regardless of speech or locality, have clearly defined clan groups which are exogamous with descent in the female line. The Pima and the Papago have a quite different social system. There are five divisions which run through all the villages of both tribes. Three of these divisions are grouped and known as the red ants or red people, and the remaining two as white ants. To the red group belong the Akol, Apap, and Apuki: to the white, Maam and Vaaf. This division of all the people into two groups gives us the moiety arrangement which is found among some of the Rio Grande Pueblos. Such dual groups are usually prominent in religious ceremonies and in games where one moiety competes with the other. There is very scanty information concerning the duties or functions of the five divisions or of the two groups to which these divisions belong. Descent in the divisions is from father to son, but we are assured that there are no marriage restrictions associated with these divisions. It is said

that members of expeditions going for salt used to paint
their faces to indicate whether they were of the red or
white moiety. That such divisions and groups formerly
had some important relation to the social or religious
life of the people must be assumed.

The families are made up of the parents, their
children, and the wives and children of the sons. This
it will be noticed is the reverse of the custom of the
Pueblo people, among whom the married daughter
remains at home. The houses, each of which is occupied
by one of these extended families, are grouped into
villages of considerable size. Each village has a chief
and a council that govern it. The official announce-
ments are made from a housetop by a village crier. The
chief and council also have a regular messenger who
summons the citizens to appear when their attendance
is desired. There is also a village officer who is in charge
of the ceremonies and festivals of the village.

The villages of the Papago are grouped into four
territorial districts to each of which a name is assigned.
The Pima appear to have two geographical groups: the
Pima of the Gila, and the Kohatk. The chiefs of the
various Pima villages elect a chief of the entire tribe who
holds office for life or until he is disabled. In an election
the son of a former chief seems to be given special consideration. The duties of the head chief appear to be
vague but his influence may be great without his powers being defined.

Leadership in war seems to have devolved upon any
individual who commanded sufficient confidence to
recruit a band to follow him, but the leadership was
only for the one expedition. Wars were waged against
the Apache and the Yuma. The Pima acted against
the Apache as a tribe rather than by villages.

## GAMES

The Pima and Papago play games similar to those of the other Southwestern people. There are two dice games. The one played by men employs four stones and that of the women eight. The points of the men's game are tallied by moving a counter about a large rectangle of stones on the ground. The Apache use a much smaller and circular space.

The guessing game is played with four reeds in one of which a bean or ball of gum is hidden. Count is kept by means of kernels of corn, one hundred being used. This is the game usually called moccasin game. It is also played by the Navajo and Apache who employ piles of dirt or a row of small holes dug in the ground.

The women play a shinny game using two connected balls which must not be touched with the hands. The purpose of the game is to carry and throw this ball over the opponent's goal line by the use of a willow stick.

There are several games of shooting with the bow and arrow intended probably to develop skill. They are for the most part confined to boys.

The races, which the pueblo dwellers make a part of their religious ceremonies, the Pima and Papago maintain with a less evident ceremonial connection. They have both the long distance race in which a ball is kicked for miles and the relay race in which two large groups of racers, representing opposing villages or large communities, compete. The relay race may be won by speed or, if the speed is nearly equal, by the superior endurance of the combined contestants on one side.

### RELIGION

When the religious activities and the ceremonial objects of the Pima and Papago are considered they are found to be much less complicated and impressive than are those of the Pueblo peoples. It seems that each village has a ceremonial house, which is of the same general structure but larger than the dwellings. Its name is "large house." The house is under the care of a man called the Keeper of the Smoke, the reference being to tobacco smoking, not to a house fire. It is not clear from the accounts, but it is to be inferred, that this man is the priestly head of the village.

There are two classes of priests, fairly distinct from each other. The Siatcokam deal with sickness and the Makai with weather and the growth of crops and with warfare. The healing priests are men and women who are selected by inheritance. The Makai are generally men who are believed to be possessed of supernatural power which enables them to perform magical acts. The production of rain is accomplished mainly by sympathetic magic, the nature of which is concealed from the observers. The spectators will be apparently sprinkled by means of dry feathers, the reeds containing the water being concealed. The novices who wish to become priests of this sort undergo a training lasting from two to four years, during which time certain restrictions are observed.

At the time of the harvest festival of the Papago certain men wear masks and are the singers of the ceremony. They are called Uipinyim and are, in a certain sense, priests. Not only are the orders of priests fewer than among the Zuñi and Hopi, but the formal organization into priesthoods seems to be lacking.

The Pueblo peoples spend much time in performing a great number and variety of ceremonies. The Papago, as far as we are informed, have only three important ceremonies. In mid-spring a ceremony is held to procure good crops of giant cactus fruit during the coming season. In July, when the giant cactus fruit is ripe, a festival of wine drinking is held. If the crops are bountiful, a harvest festival is sometimes celebrated in the Santa Rosa Valley, Arizona.

This ceremony, called Vigita, is the joint performance of the five villages of the valley. The exact date is fixed at the meeting of a council held at one of the villages. Preparations are immediately begun for the festival. On the eve of the tenth day before the main celebration a large bundle of feathered sticks which have been made for the occasion is placed in the center of the feast ground. The men gather around this bundle and listen to two formulated speeches which recite the origin and previous celebrations of the Vigita. Ten tally sticks are stuck in the ground, one of which is pulled up and carried away each evening, so that the number of days may be accurately kept. The next night messengers are sent to the various villages to announce the date of the festival. Songs are composed and practised for the coming celebration. Each village has eight chief singers, each one of whom composes a song. These are taught to the other singers of that village and to those constituting the village chorus who are not composers of songs. The masks of the singers are made of gourds which are painted in colors with designs representing lightning, clouds, and grains of corn. A second set of performers have large cloth masks to which tin disks and turkey feathers are fastened. There are designs on the masks representing clouds. They carry crude bows and arrows and long poles with which the fruit of the giant cactus is knocked down. The men themselves are said to represent the giant cactus. They are called clowns and appear as such, but since they are also the attendants of the singers and the head men it is proper to assume that, as is the case among the Pueblo people, the duties of these apparent clowns are of considerable importance.

The main celebration occupies one day and takes place in an enclosure about 30 feet square made of wattling. In the center of the enclosure is a forked post on which is placed a basket of cornmeal. To the east of the post is a flat cotton emblem of the sun and to the west a similar one of the moon. The enclosure is subdivided so that each village has its own plot wherein sacred objects are placed and where the singers for the particular village gather. Near each of these enclosures miniature fields are made of sand representing the arroyo which contributes the water, the irrigation ditches, and the fields themselves. These are cared for by the clowns.

The day of the festival all those in attendance are sprinkled with cornmeal to keep away sickness. Each adult takes a feathered stick, puts cornmeal on it, and brushes himself as a cleansing rite. The men of the respective villages, each for himself, have made of twigs a representation of some food products, clouds, game animals, and cotton. At noon these are carried to the village plot within the enclosure. As they move toward the spot bullroarers are swung, representing the sound of rain.

During the afternoon songs are sung. When darkness has fallen well-informed old men dressed as clowns deliver set speeches. After the speechmaking each village in order sings the songs which have been practised during the period of preparation. Two of the singers from each village, wearing special masks, represent the corn. The singing occupies the night. Just before dawn all the singers remove their clothing and paint their bodies with spots to represent the multi-colored corn. Just as the sun rises two men, one bearing the symbol of the sun and the other the symbol of the moon, pass out through the opening of the enclosure, toward the east. Here they are met by two pairs of boys and girls representing the children who were once sacrificed. Old men scrape notched sticks with a shoulder-blade and sing while the children dance.

During the day the ceremonial objects which have been prepared as mentioned above are paraded. The singers continue their songs and the clowns imitate shamans performing magic, and impersonate men drunk with giant cactus wine. Toward night when all the objects have been shown, each village sings four songs, different from those previously sung, and the festival is over.

There were ceremonial activities connected with hunting and warfare. We have the statement that the Pima, after killing an enemy, observed so many restrictions and for so long a time that their usefulness as scouts was impaired. The salt expeditions to the Gulf of California are conducted according to the pattern of war expeditions with offerings and ceremonial restrictions.

There are numerous shrines in the country of the Pima and Papago; some of them on mountain tops and others in caves. The offerings deposited at these shrines differed; at some of them twigs were placed and at others arrows.

As is the case with the pueblo dwellers, the religious ceremonies, the means employed with the hope of influencing events, consist of songs and of objects and activities of a magical character.

The beliefs of the Pima and Papago in regard to the supernatural fall rather naturally into those concerning the more striking manifestations of nature such as lightning, thunder, the sun and moon, wind, and rain on the one hand; and the conception of superhuman personalities such as Earth Magician, who was the Creator, and Elder Brother, who appeared later on the scene, but ultimately superseded Earth Magician and became the Culture Hero.

The Creator, or Earth Magician, alone, was floating on darkness until he rubbed cuticle from his body which, by the aid of the white ants he had created, became the earth. Later there was a flood from the effects of which the main personages were saved. Elder Brother killed a monster eagle which was preying upon humanity. Earth Magician on leaving this upper world shed certain impurities from his body which are responsible for sickness and other human ills.

The Pima and Papago during the ceremonies repeat portions of these myths and sing songs of the supernatural persons and animals both ancient and modern. The religious beliefs and practices of the Pima and Papago are closely similar to those of the pueblo dwellers, but are less elaborate and spectacular.

# CHAPTER IV

# THE CAMP DWELLERS

THE camp dwellers may be called nomadic. Their houses are so constructed that they require only a minimum amount of labor and material so that they are readily abandoned and easily replaced by others set up in another location. They depend comparatively little upon agriculture and therefore are not permanently bound to the locality of their fields and storerooms. The securing of their wild food, both animal and vegetable, requires considerable traveling about.

## DISTRIBUTION

These people belonged to two linguistic stocks: the Athapascan, consisting of the Navajo and several Apache tribes; and the Yuman, which includes the Walapai, Yavapai, and Havasupai.

*Athapascan.* The Athapascan tribes in the eastern portion of the territory speak languages related to the Déné of the north, in the Mackenzie and Yukon valleys, and to the various scattered bands in western Oregon and northwestern California. The name Apache was widely applied by both the Spaniards, and the Americans who succeeded them, to several distinct tribes.

In the northeast are the Jicarilla Apache, who are again divided into two bands. One of these, the Llanero, lived on the headwaters of the Canadian River and in the mountains between that stream and the Rio Grande. The Ollero lived west of the Rio Grande, especially along the Chama River.

In the mountains between the Rio Pecos and the Rio Grande, south of White Mountain, were the Mescalero Apache. They consisted of many bands, each of which claimed a rather definite locality as its home. The territory occupied by them extended southward to the mouth of the Pecos, but the bands in the lower part of this region were less closely allied to the Mescalero proper in political feeling and there was a slight difference in dialect. West of the Rio Grande in the valley of the Mimbres was an Apache tribe now nearly extinct. They formerly were called the Mimbreños, but are better known by the name of their great war leader, Victorio. When he was defeated a part of this band joined the Mescalero and others united with the tribes west of them. The Apache living on the headwaters of the Gila River and southward are known as the Chiricahua. This tribe really consisted of four almost independent bands, each with a chief. These are the Indians who have made the name of Apache so widely known. They had robbed the Mexican settlements for many years before the American occupation. When later they were deprived of their native lands and placed on a reservation, they fled to Mexico where they lived by plundering on either side of the international boundary line. Their most noted chiefs were Mangas Coloradas, Whoa, Cochise, and Geronimo. The last named with the larger part of this band surrendered to General Miles in 1886. They were taken to Florida with their families as prisoners of war. After less than a year they were removed to Alabama and finally were given a place on a reservation at Fort Sill, Oklahoma.

The name San Carlos has been applied to the Apache bands gathered on a reservation of that name. They formerly lived on the San Carlos River, on the Gila River near the mouth of San Carlos, on Arivaipa

Creek which flows into the San Pedro, a southern tributary of the Gila, and about certain springs north and west of the town of Globe, Arizona.

On White River and other upper tributaries of the Salt River, were a number of bands of Apache quite similar in all respects to those last mentioned. These have often been called the Coyotero because they were looked upon as wild, but are now generally spoken of as the White Mountain Apache.

The Salt River receives a considerable tributary called Tonto Creek from the north. Near the head of this stream is a large valley known as Tonto Basin which was occupied by a tribe so well isolated from other Apache that a dialectic difference in language was developed. They were closely associated with the Yavapai who are Yuman in their speech. These two groups were placed on the San Carlos Reservation in 1875 where they remained until 1905.

The Navajo, called by the Spanish "Apaches de Navajo," occupy nearly all the region between the San Juan and the Little Colorado rivers and roam far outside of that territory in all directions. In language they are not very different from the Western Apache, but in culture they are fairly distinct, being mainly a pastoral people. Just prior to the American occupation, they were almost constantly raiding the Mexican settlements of New Mexico. They killed their first Indian agent and resisted American control. A large number of the tribe were taken prisoners and removed in 1864 to Fort Sumner on the Pecos River where they were confined for four years.

*Yuman.* The western portion of Arizona and the lower Colorado River Valley are occupied by tribes speaking Yuman languages. The Maricopa, a Yuman-speaking people, are mentioned above as living with the Pima. They are believed to have left the lower Colorado not many generations ago. North of the Maricopa, along the Rio Verde and eastward toward the Tonto Basin, are the Yavapai, often called the Mohave-Apache. They have acquired the latter name because of their close association with the Apache, to whom their relation is analogous to that existing between the Maricopa and the Pima. In Cataract Canyon, a branch of the Grand Canyon, the Havasupai live during the summer. They are in friendly relations with the Hopi and in trading relations with the Navajo. To the west of the Havasupai on the plateau south of the Colorado River and north of Bill Williams Creek are the Walapai.

Between the Rio Verde and the Colorado, west of the country of the Yavapai, formerly lived a tribe popularly called Yuma Apache, for whom the name Tulkepaia is also known. They were placed on the San Carlos Reservation in 1875, and seem to have merged with the Yavapai with whom they had a common language.

## Shelters

These nomadic tribes do not show a great degree of uniformity either in their material culture or in their religion. We shall find their houses, their methods of securing food, and their social habits changing as we pass from tribe to tribe.

Both of the eastern bands of the Apache, the Jicarilla and the Mescalero, live in skin or cloth-covered tipis which differ in no important respect from those used by the Plains Indians. The Mescalero sometimes make brush shelters as well, and perhaps always made a practice of using them when they were in the mountains.

When on the treeless plains nothing was so desirable as the easily portable conical dwelling of skins or canvas.

All of the Apache west of the Rio Grande made houses which had frames of poles, covered with a thatch of weeds or grass. The prevailing type among the San Carlos Apache is dome-shaped. When the house is small, the frame is made by setting poles a

San Carlos Apache Women building a House

few inches in the ground in a circle, bending their tops over, and lashing them together. These poles are held in the proper curves by horizontal ones lashed to them. When a larger house is needed, poles are first placed forming a series of arches which overlap each other and together complete a circle except for the doorway. These arches support the main ribs running from the ground to the apex. The thatch, which is usually bear grass, is applied in regular, overlapping courses and is bound in place with strips of yucca leaves. The White Mountain Apache houses frequently have two long sloping sides meeting in a line above, like an ordinary gable roof. In recent years, cornstalks and the limbs of trees are frequently used for thatching with the additional protection of a strip of canvas.

White Mountain Apache House

The Tonto Apache and the Yuma peoples build houses with a somewhat conical shape. The houses of the Havasupai have four important posts coming to a peak which furnish the foundation. Other smaller poles are leaned between these on which a thatch is applied. Earth is piled around the bottom and in winter nearly to the top in order to shed the rain. The doorway in winter faces the sunrise at that season, a little south of west. The houses of the Walapai are said to be less substantial than those of the Havasupai.

The Navajo live in winter in earth-covered lodges. The house has for its chief support three large logs with forked tops. These are locked together by placing the fork of one in the fork of a second, and thrusting the fork of the third between them. Other logs and small poles are laid on these until a conical house is enclosed. Brush is placed in the larger cracks and

Navajo House

earth is piled on to a depth of several inches. Such a house leaks only after a long, hard rain. A doorway is made on the east side and between the doorway and the apex a large hole is left to admit light and air and through which the smoke may escape. Six-sided houses are also built of logs placed horizontally. By drawing them in gradually after the walls have been carried to a proper height, the roof is formed. A smoke hole is left at the apex. During the summer the Navajo generally camp with only a shelter of brush or a stone wall to protect them from the prevailing winds.

## FOOD SUPPLY

The nomadic tribes had a large territory at their disposal. There were fertile and fairly well-watered river valleys where corn and beans could be raised, and vast tracts of upland covered, if sparsely, with a varied vegetation. Judging from the number of cattle and sheep which that region now supports, before their introduction there must have been sufficient food for many deer, antelope, and elk. A few days' travel east from the Rio Grande were the buffalo plains with a supply of meat limited only by the means of transporting it.

Corn was planted by all the tribes; but the Eastern Apache, the Jicarilla and Mescalero, depended but little upon agriculture. That the Navajo formerly had large fields was stated by Benavides, who gave that fact as the explanation of their name. The methods employed seem not to differ particularly from those of the village Indians. The corn is planted in irregularly spaced bunches, rather than in rows. The Navajo cornfields are in the moist valleys. The White Mountain Apache plant their fields in river beds wherever the streams have left a fertile flat. Sometimes the water is turned on these by diverting it into simple ditches with a log placed in the edge of the stream.

The Havasupai, being located in Cataract Canyon, have exceptional opportunities for agriculture. The canyon walls broaden out, making a valley nearly two and a half miles long. Over this valley the water of the creek is conducted by means of ditches in the sand and slight dams across the stream. The light soil and sudden rises in the stream level make it necessary frequently to renew both ditches and dams. To the fertile soil and a plentiful water supply is added summer heat, since the valley is a half mile lower than the surrounding plateau. Peaches and figs are now raised, besides the native crops, maize, beans, and squash. When the crops have been harvested, they are dried and stored in caves and small storage rooms.

The country of the Walapai is unsuited to agriculture. There are only scattered spots with sufficient moisture to permit the raising of crops.

Apache Woman gathering Mescal

The nomadic people make extensive use of the wild vegetable products. The piñon produces large crops of nuts which the woodrats gather. It is only necessary to rob their nests to secure an abundant supply. The mesquite grows in most localities and furnishes edible pods when they are green and later bean-like seeds which are pounded into flour. The amole, *Yucca baccata*, has a banana-shaped fruit which is cooked in the ashes, and may then be dried for later use. The agave, a century plant, furnishes a large bulk of nutritious food. The plants are watched until signs of the flowering stalk appear when they are seven or eight years old. The entire plant is severed near the base by means of a chisel-shaped stick which is hammered with a stone. The plant is then turned top down and trimmed with a broad knife of native manufacture. A leaf or two is left for a handle by which the stumps are carried to a large deep pit used year after year.

Mescal Knife.    San Carlos Apache

This pit is thoroughly heated and filled with stumps. A covering of earth is thrown over them and a fire maintained on top for a day or more. The cooked material is dried in the sun and packed in bales for transportation to the camp. This food, while coarse, is not unpalatable.

There are many species of cacti, most of which have edible fruit. The giant cactus, which grows on the lower elevations, because of its great size yields abundantly. The fruit is pressed into large balls which keep indefinitely. These contain many black seeds which are separated by soaking and ground for flour. There are many berries, seeds of grasses and sunflowers, nuts, and bulbs, which add considerably to the required food supply.

The Eastern Apache made regular trips to the buffalo plains, at the time of the year when the buffalo were driven south by the cold. They killed a large number, dried the meat, and packed it in bags, or parfleches, made of the hides of the animals killed. These were tied on the backs of horses for transportation.

Men went out singly to hunt deer and antelope wearing a headdress with the horns of the animals that they might approach them more readily. There were communal hunts for elk particularly. The leader of the hunt placed the men at the points that commanded the passageways and trails, and the animals were driven toward them. Corrals were also used into which the antelope were driven.

The Athapascan tribes never eat fish nor waterfowl. The taboo is explained by the Indians as due to a fear of water which is connected with the thunder.

The Havasupai move to the plateau above their canyon after their harvest and spend the fall and winter in gathering wild foods and in hunting deer, mountain-sheep, and formerly antelope. They are thus furnished with a plentiful supply of flesh to be eaten with their corn. The surplus skins are dressed and traded to other tribes.

For some years before and after the American occupation of the region, the Western Apache and the Navajo lived to a large extent on the cattle, sheep, horses, mules, and burros they were able to drive off from the settlements.

Both tribes seem to have undertaken the breeding of horses a long time ago. The Apache have attempted cattle raising only recently. Their burial customs formerly required the destruction of all personal property at the death of the owner, and that his herds be slaughtered. Recently the Apache herds have increased and go far toward supplying the necessary flesh diet. The Navajo, apparently without foreign instruction, began the rearing of sheep a century or more ago. Sheep raising has become an important industry and has worked great changes in their culture. It has largely superseded hunting and, to a considerable extent, agriculture.

## CLOTHING

The Jicarilla Apache wore buckskin clothing similar to that of the Plains. The Mescalero and the Western Apache women had dresses in two parts. The upper garment had an opening for the head and two large square portions which fell in front and behind to the hips. A skirt reached from the waist to the knees and was generously provided with fringes of buckskin. Less is known of the men's clothing. It seems to have been scanty, except on festive occasions and in winter. A shirt and leggings were probably worn, with a skin robe for winter.

The Navajo men sometimes wore shirts and trousers with full length legs of buckskin. These were variously colored by dyeing, usually green or red. When cloth became more easily procurable, white cotton trousers with the lower part of the legs slit on the outer side were adopted. The upper garment was preferably of velveteen and answered the purpose of both shirt and blouse. A handkerchief or colored strip of cloth is worn about the head to confine the hair. The moccasins, which are colored brown, come up around the ankle where they are fastened by a silver button. The robe, until recently, was the woolen blanket manufactured by the Navajo women, of the type now generally called a "chief."

Mescalero Girl in Native Costume

The women wore a dress consisting of two rectangular pieces of woolen goods sewed up the sides and part away across one end, openings being left for the neck and arms. The decorations of these dresses were of a peculiar sort, restricted to the two ends and sym-

Navajo Man
(Photo by Howard McCormick)

metrically arranged.   Knitted leggings of black wool
were worn and buckskin moccasins over these.

Both men and women wear much silver jewelry of
native manufacture.   Necklaces and belts are the
most elaborate, but the bracelets and the finger rings
set with turquoise are attractively made.

## INDUSTRIAL ARTS

*Pottery.*   All these people appear originally to have
made unpainted pottery.   The Jicarilla Apache and the
Navajo still make what is required for household
purposes.   The Jicarilla in former days were rather
noted for the excellent cooking pots which they made.
Their ware was seldom painted, the decoration consisting of ridges or series of points modeled in low relief
usually near the rim.   The vessels are molded in a
similar manner to that employed by the Pueblo peoples,
but they are fired with pine bark which gives them a
lusterless black surface.   As the pots cool they are
coated with piñon gum which is said to prevent their
breaking.

The Navajo make vessels similar in appearance.
They are usually cylindrical in shape and with buckskin stretched over them are used for drums in ceremonies.

*Basketry.*   It is in basketry that the mechanical and
artistic skill of the nomadic peoples is best displayed.
The baskets of both the Jicarilla and the Mescalero are
quite different from those made by the Western Apache,
the Yavapai, and the Pima.   The Jicarilla baskets are
of the coiled or sewed variety.   The foundation is of
three, or sometimes five, twigs of sumac or willow.   The
sewing material is made from similar twigs by splitting
them into three parts and separating the sap wood from
the heart.   The sap portion, which is the part that is

used, is trimmed to the proper size, and that required for designs is dyed. The old dyes were made from the root bark of the mountain mahogany, which gives red, and the root of the barberry, which gives yellow. At the present time aniline dyes are used and the colors are gaudy and varied.

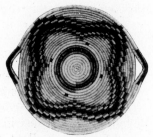

Jicarilla Tray

The patterns are geometrical: triangles, rectangles, and bands. The names of these designs indicate that they represent certain natural objects such as mountains, houses, plots of ground, trails, and gates. It is seldom, however, that they are combined in such a way as to make a connected composition. The Jicarilla at the present time make almost no use of baskets except for water jars. These are made of close coiling in the shape of a jug. The inside is coated with piñon pitch which has had its consistency reduced by boiling. This renders the vessel water-tight and also provides an easily cleaned surface. The outside is kept white by frequent applications of white earth. Two loops of leather or hair are made on one side through which the carrying strap passes.

San Carlos Apache Tray

The Mescalero also make coiled baskets, but since they use two rods placed one above the other in each coil of the foundation, the baskets have wide thin coils. Above the rods are placed two or more strips of leaves to serve as a welt. The material used for sewing is chiefly obtained by splitting the leaves of the narrow-leaved yucca. These are used green, partly bleached to a yellow, or entirely bleached to white. A red material

Mescalero Unfinished Basket

is obtained from the root of the yucca. These decorated baskets are made principally for sale, although they are used to some extent for storage. The water jars are similar in shape to those made by the Jicarilla, but they are frequently pitched on the outside as well as

inside.   Burden or carrying baskets are still in common
use.   They are made by varied processes of twining
which produce decorative effects.   The material most
desired is mulberry, the twigs of which are exceedingly
durable.   In most cases the women do not assign such
names to the designs as would lead one to think the
patterns are intended to be symbolic.   One old woman,

Jicarilla Water Basket and San Carlos Apache Burden and Storage
Baskets

however, pointed out on a very crude basket the milky
way, morningstar, and a rainbow.   These particular
things are considered very sacred;   and in spite of the
denials of many of the women it is probable that Mescalero baskets do often have symbols on them which are
expected to benefit the users of the baskets.

The Arizona Apache and Yavapai make baskets
in black and white almost exclusively.   The baskets are
coiled on a three-rod foundation, either of aromat-

ic sumac or willow. The warp or sewing material is of sumac, willow, or cottonwood, and is prepared as has been described above. No dyes are employed; but for black, the outer portion of the dried pods of the martynia, sometimes called devil's claw, is used. The patterns are continuous, radiating from the center in zigzags or in bands encircling the basket. The designs are often geometrical and apparently are not symbolic. There are many baskets with zigzag lines which usually have names referring to the lightning. It is probable that considerable feeling and importance attach to such designs. The Yavapai perhaps produce the more beautiful baskets, frequently depicting men and animals conventionalized to meet the requirements of basket work. The carrying baskets of the Western Apache are twined and are made of the same materials employed by the Mescalero. In twining, two rods of the foundation are enclosed each time between the twists of the twining strands. Strips and fringes of buckskin are used on these baskets for further ornamentation. The water jars are twined and coated with red ocher and finely pounded juniper leaves before the piñon pitch is applied. This pitch is first reduced in consistency by boiling, which requires great care to prevent the distilling vapor from taking fire. The pitch is applied to both the interior and the outer surface of the vessels.

The baskets of the Havasupai and Walapai are similar, but are less skillfully made and not so finely ornamented.

*Weaving.* It is not known that any of the camp-dwelling peoples raised cotton or wove cloth before the Spanish period.

That sheep were introduced into the Southwest in the seventeenth century we know, for certain of the Rio Grande villages are credited with flocks of sheep at

the time of the rebellion in 1680.  The Navajo were
the only people to undertake the raising of sheep on
a considerable scale and to turn to a pastoral life.

When blankets are to be made from the wool, it
is sorted, spread out on a sloping stone, and then washed

Navajo Woman Spinning

by pouring hot water containing an extract of the yucca
root over it.  The carding is done with a pair of ordinary European hand cards and there is no evidence of
a more primitive means ever having been employed.
The spindle, however, is the same as that found in cliff

ruins. It consists of a small stick at the base of which
is a wooden disk to give momentum and facilitate the
winding of the yarn.

Navajo Woman beating Down the Woof with a Batten Stick

The loom is a simple frame in which the warp is
placed vertically. The weaving is from the bottom
upward, the blanket being lowered as the work progres-
ses. No shuttle is used, the yarn being inserted with
the fingers or with the aid of a small stick. The woof
is forced down by pressure with a fork or by the blow

of a batten stick.  The weaving is peculiar in that the woof strands of a particular color are not carried entirely across the blanket, but only as far as that color is required for the design.  They are then dropped and another color is taken up.

In plain weaving the warp is divided into two divisions or sheds by attaching alternate threads by means of loops of yarn to two small sticks.  The sheds or sets of warp strands are separated by pushing down

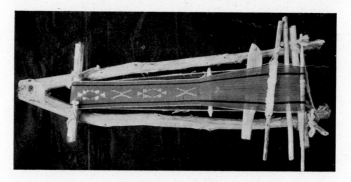

Navajo Belt Loom

a small rod and twisting the batten stick and are crossed by pulling up on the stick to which the loops are attached.

Diagonal weaving is accomplished by making four instead of two sheds.  By this means paired strands of the warp can be lifted and a raised pattern is made with a slope to one side or the other.  By still other groupings of the warp, diamonds are produced.  This style of weaving is used particularly in saddle blankets.

Sashes are woven on a similar loom which, since it is small, is stretched on a forked stick or by fastening one end to a tree and the other to the waist of the weaver.

The patterns are varied by causing the warp instead of the woof to appear in the desired places.

The colors employed are the natural white and brown of the well-washed wool, a gray which results from the mingling of these, and various native and commercial dyes. They produce black by combining a concoction of sumac (*Rhus aromatica*), roasted ocher, and piñon gum. Dull red was obtained by placing the

Navajo Chief Blanket

yarn in a liquid made by boiling the bark of alder and mountain mahogany in water. Lemon yellow was secured by the use of the yellow flowers of the shrubby *Bigelovia graveolens* and a native alum. Old gold resulted from rubbing into the wool a paste made of sorrel roots and crude alum ground together. In rather early days indigo for blue was obtained from the Mexicans and displaced an earlier native blue. A bright scarlet and a

Navajo Blanket.   Sage Collection

rose color were obtained in the early history of blanket-making by cutting or raveling woolen cloth obtained from Europeans. Blankets containing such material are called "bayeta" from the Spanish name of flannel used in the soldiers' uniforms. There were a few years during which the Navajo frequently bought yarn ready spun and dyed from the traders. These blankets are usually called Germantowns.

Some of the earliest examples of Navajo weaving have horizontal stripes running across the web. The so-called chief's blankets, in addition to these stripes have a diamond in the center and portions of one at the corners and the middle of each side. Others also called chief's and woven to serve as robes for wearing, have three parallelograms running through the middle and at either end. If these blankets are folded the halves and quarters are identical in decoration. When designs are introduced which do not run entirely across the web the colored yarns are dropped at the margins of the design and other colors taken up. This is tapestry weaving, difficult to imitate by machinery.

The more common design units are squares, parallelograms, diamonds, and triangles. Diamonds are often formed by intersecting diagonal lines which run across the blanket, half diamonds resulting at the sides. The outlines of the figures in many cases are broken with right angles, that is, consist of a series of steps. These designs have descriptive Navajo names, such as "sling" for the elongated diamond, "three points" for the triangle. The ordinary diamond is called "star large," by which the morningstar is meant. This and the zigzag line representing lightning and triangular masses called clouds have more or less religious connotation and may be symbolic in their intention.

It is assumed that the Navajo, who formerly did not weave, learned the art from their Pueblo neighbors who are known to have practised it in prehistoric times. They seem to have taken over the loom and the general methods of preparing the yarn and weaving it. The practice of making designs in colors which do not cross the entire width of the blanket seems to have originated with the Navajo. This method of making the design while the weaving is in progress is similar to that with which they were familiar in basket making.

*Silverwork.* The art of metal working is certainly an introduced one in the Southwest. It is practised by many tribes in North America, usually with the softer metals like German silver. The Navajo, however, use Mexican silver coins and have become very expert. Most of the work is done by pounding the material on a small anvil with an ordinary steel hammer. A small forge with bellows is used to soften the metal and to melt it when it is necessary to make casts in molds. The hammered pieces are decorated by stamping designs on them with steel dies which are prepared by the Navajo themselves.

The products are finger rings set with turquoise matrix, bracelets, large oval disks for leather belts, and neck ornaments. These neck ornaments are usually a string of hollow spherical beads and a pendant consisting of two joined crescents. Between the beads are often placed conventionalized squash blossoms.

*Beadwork.* The Eastern Apache do much work with glass beads. These are either sewed to articles of leather and buckskin, such as purses, tobacco bags, awl cases, belts, and moccasins; or they are woven in a belt loom having a warp and woof of cotton thread. The beads are strung on the woof by means of two needles which pass a double thread through the beads and on either side of the warp threads. The designs are mostly geometrical, similar to those found in basket work, but realistic ones are found in which circular saws, bows and arrows, and butterflies are represented.

The Eastern Apache paint designs on rawhide bags as do the Plains Indians. They have the envelope type of receptacle known as the parfleche. The Western Apache use instead saddlebags decorated with cut designs and streamers. This art no doubt is of Spanish origin, taken over with the horse and saddle.

## SOCIAL ORGANIZATION

The Eastern Apache, as far as can be discovered, have no clans, or other divisions regulating marriage. The Western Apache and the Navajo have clans which are exogamous, regulating social duties and relations and especially marriage. The explanation of the names, which are geographical, is that in mythical times a band camped for a time at a place where a cottonwood tree stood by a stream or where some accident befell them and from this tree or circumstance, a name was given the clan. Were one to trust to these myths he would conclude that the clans represent former geographical or political groups. This does not appear to be true for the Navajo. The clans of both the Navajo and the White Mountain Apache do seem to be somewhat localized. Certain clans of the latter have numerous members residing in the western portion of the Apache territory and but few in the eastern region. The region which in the myth gives the name to the clan is in some instances definitely localized by the Apache and the clan is still associated with that region. Carrizo Creek is named in Apache Lokadigai, with reference to the reeds which grow in its bed and

which are also responsible for the Spanish name
Carrizo. One of the clans is named from this creek,
Lokadigaihn, and its members are more numerous in
this valley than in other parts of the Apache region.
Certain political bands are also associated in the Apache
mind with definite clans. Since in each family the
mother and children belong to one clan and the father
to another, there can never be localization or division
into political groups in a strict sense. In the valley of
Carrizo Creek the members of various other clans are
more numerous than are those of the one clan which is
associated with the creek by name.

The clans of the Navajo number between forty and
fifty and those of the Western Apache over thirty.
Among both tribes the clans are more or less grouped
and the entire group usually is exogamous but does not
bear a distinctive name.

## Social Customs

The young men among the Navajo and Apache in
former days secured their brides by displaying their
ability as hunters. The man came to the lodge of his
chosen maiden with a deer which he placed outside. If
her family were willing to have him as a son-in-law, the
deer was taken and eaten. The young man lived with
his father-in-law for some time and hunted for the
support of the family. A strict mother-in-law taboo
exists among the nomadic Athapascans of the Southwest. The young man must never meet his mother-in-
law. Among the Mescalero Apache the taboo extends
to the mother-in-law's sisters and mother. They are
never permitted to be in the same room together or
directly to address one another. When it is absolutely
necessary for communication to take place between

them, one shouts to the other from a distance using the third person. "Tell him to come and eat, his dinner is ready," his mother-in-law may call, and leave her lodge while the young man comes to eat. The penalty among the Apache for the infringement of this taboo is believed to be blindness inflicted by some supernatural power. The Indians assign no other reason for the existence of this restriction and probably no other is felt than that such meetings and intercourse are improper.

Among the Apache there are other minor restrictions between relations-in-law, especially in regard to the calling of their personal names. An intimate relation, implying mutual aid, exists between a man and his brother's son. Cousins whose fathers are brothers treat each other with great familiarity, often indulging in insulting remarks which must not be resented. A widow about to remarry is at the disposal of the clan of her deceased husband and she usually marries one of his brothers or near relatives.

The adult dead are buried at a distance from the camping places and the graves are covered with stones and brush. The personal property is placed at the grave and a horse or two is generally killed near by. The Jicarilla used to cut off the heads of the horses so sacrificed, as is the custom among some of the Plains tribes. Dead infants are usually wrapped in their cradles which are suspended in trees. The reason for this different treatment of children is not known but the custom has been noted in the preceding pages as a prehistoric one in this region. Great fear is shown of dead bodies and all objects associated with them. The Apache burn the houses and the Navajo desert them after a death has occurred. All the Yuman peoples seem to have practised cremation. The Havasupai

discontinued the cremation about sixty years ago;
now, the dead are buried with their favorite posses-
sions. The Walapai make annual offerings to the dead
of a particular year by a community burning of food
and clothing.

## POLITICAL ORGANIZATION

The government of the nomadic tribes is much less
formal than that of the sedentary peoples. The
Jicarilla now have a chief elected from each of the two
bands. One of these is recognized by the Agency
officials and by the Indians themselves as tribal chief.
In earlier times the two divisions appear to have been
politically independent, each having chiefs of coördi-
nate rank. Both war and hunting parties were under
the control of a head man who directed them. While
it is probable that the same individual frequently
acted in this capacity it is not certain that the office
of war chief was definitely bestowed.

The Western Apache are divided into many small
bands each with a chief who holds office for life and
who is frequently succeeded by his son if he proves
himself efficient. The office seems to have been bestowed by common consent. One of the main duties
of the chief is to address his people each morning about
dawn, keeping them informed as to past or future
events of community interest.

The Navajo at the present time appear to be without
any formal native government except that organized
for them by the Indian Department. Originally there
were recognized chiefs both for war and peace. That the
entire Navajo country was under the control of the
same officials does not seem possible. It seems more
likely that each locality had its own leaders.

The Navajo and the Apache bands united in common action against other tribes and against the Mexicans and Americans under the leadership of such men as had proved themselves capable leaders. As examples may be mentioned Geronimo who led several bands of the Apache for a number of years and Manuelito, among the Navajo, who led them in their fight against the Americans.

### GAMES

The Apache and Navajo have several games which are played partly for amusement but largely in the hope of gain. As elsewhere in North America, these games have a semi-religious character. There is a

Hoop and Pole Game.   Apache

myth which explains their origin and songs and prayers to bring about success in playing. Most dignity is attached among the Apache to the hoop and pole game. The implements employed are a hoop with incised bands and a string stretched along the diameter in which many knots are tied and two long poles, the larger ends of which have a number of incised bands. To play it two men stand side by side at one end of a level stretch of ground. One rolls the hoop down this stretch and both throw the poles after it. If the hoop falls on the butt of one of the poles a count is made according to the knots of the string or the incised rings which happen to be in contact with the rings cut into the pole. The incised rings are named for the lightning and the hoop represents a snake. Women are never allowed to witness the playing of this game. The Navajo game is similar.

A guessing game is played by a number of players divided into two parties. A man representing one of these parties hides a ball in one of several piles of sand or in a moccasin. The other party must guess its location.

The women play a game with three split staves which are dropped vertically on a stone. There are several counts according to the position in which they fall. If the split side of all three sticks is up, the count is five, but if the rounded side of all three is up, the count is ten. The score of the game is kept by moving a stick for each player around a circle marked by forty small stones. There are openings at four points, called rivers. If the stick of a player falls into a river she must return it to the beginning place again. A similar game is played by the men.

## RELIGION

*Ceremonies.* The religious practices of the nomadic peoples have much in common with those of the Pueblos. They make sand or dry paintings, those of the Navajo being very numerous and very elaborate. Individuals, masked or otherwise distinguished, represent divine persons in the ceremonies. Pollen is strewed and is the regular accompaniment of prayers. The Navajo make use of prayer offerings and also have fetishes which are used both in hunting and in the care of their flocks and herds. The Apache make much use of sacred beads and feathers which are worn about the person, on the wrists, or as a bandolier across the breast.

A ceremony held for girls when they attain womanhood is considered of prime importance among the Apache tribes and has been maintained while other ceremonies have fallen into neglect. The essential features of this ceremony are numerous songs and prayers uttered by the priest hired for the occasion, dancing by the girl or girls for whom it is held, a foot race by the girl, and the painting of the girl and of the spectators, who expect good fortune as a result.

The Jicarilla ceremony is peculiar in that a boy is associated with a girl in the ceremony. He is called Naiyenezgani and the girl Esdzanadlehi. These names are those of the culture hero and his grandmother, but they are undoubtedly associated also with the sun and the moon.

The Apache of Arizona hold ceremonies of varying degrees of elaboration. Every girl on reaching maturity is secluded and subject to certain restrictions, especially in regard to touching her lips to water and scratching her person with her nails.

For most girls a morning ceremony is held. A priest or professional singer is employed who with his helpers forms a chorus. About dawn this chorus stands in a line facing the east and the girl takes her place in front of it. Many songs are sung of the creation of the world and the first adolescence ceremony. The girl dances; first standing, and then on her knees. Later, she lies prone while a matron kneads and pulls her into comely proportions. The assembled spectators sprinkle the girl with pollen and ask that she may have a fortunate life. The girl runs certain races after which her family serves a feast.

The Apache Ceremony for an Adolescent Girl
Above: the Morning Ceremony
Below: the Dancing Gans.   Ash Greek, Arizona

A second ceremony is often held at night. Four poles properly marked with symbols are set up to form a pyramid which is conceived as a lodge. Within this structure at night a long series of songs is sung by a chorus seated near a small fire. The girl, one of her associates, and two boys of similar age stand and dance with their faces toward the east. Special songs are sung at dawn. During the morning, first the girl and then the spectators are painted with white earth.

Jicarilla Relay Race

Frequently a priest is hired who presents four men dressed to represent gods called Gans. A fifth man acts as a clown. These gods appear at twilight and return at intervals during the evening and early morning. They enter in a processional and then dance about a large fire. They go through certain conventional steps and movements and present a most impressive and weird spectacle with the play of the firelight on their blackened bodies and decorated headdresses. These gods return in the morning and assist in the painting ceremony described above.

These ceremonies on the whole have a festive as well as a religious character. The purposes may be considered to be in part the bringing to the notice of suitors and others that the girl is now marriageable and to insure for her a long and happy life.

The Jicarilla have an annual festival which resembles very closely that held at Taos. The entire tribe camps near a large lake in the southwestern corner of their reservation. The two bands, the Llanero and the Ollero, pitch their tipis on opposite sides. On the day preceding the public festival, the young men of each band, accompanied by the older men, go some distance from the camp and hold a preliminary race by which those who are to run in the final race are chosen. Two booths are constructed, one at either end of the race course. From these the two bands issue in irregular bunches surrounding a drum. The dancers have cottonwood branches in their hands and are led by a man carrying a standard from which flies a cotton cloth and on the top of which are two ears of corn. The two bands of dancers approach each other and pass, each going to the goal of the other. During the night and the early morning, ceremonies are held in the booths, a sand painting is made, the racers are painted, and prayers are said for them by priests. About noon the relay race takes place, practically under the same conditions and in the same manner as has already been described for Taos.

The Jicarilla have a healing ceremony held at the request of someone who is ill. A large space is enclosed by a brush fence. At one end of this a tipi or a booth is set up. Within this a sand painting is drawn representing many animals. A buffalo skin is stretched over a pit and beaten like a drum, the moccasins of the patient being used for drumsticks.

The shoulder blade of a deer or antelope is rubbed over a notched stick producing considerable noise. Rattles are also used as an accompaniment to loud singing. This singing and noise are intended to scare away the evil influence which has resulted from the patient's having crossed the tracks of a bear or rattlesnake. Within the brush enclosure a dance is held at night. Men painted in two styles and decorated with fir boughs come in and perform many apparent miracles such as making corn increase in a pot and taking rabbits from a seemingly empty vessel. These two sets of dancers probably correspond to the cuirana and the koshare of the Rio Grande Pueblos. The Ute hold a ceremony similar to this each spring known as the bear dance.

The Navajo have developed many elaborate ceremonies each of which is under the control of a school of priests, the numbers of which are maintained by those who apply for initiation and training. These ceremonies for the most part are held at the request and expense of some individual who is ill or indisposed.

A special conical lodge of logs covered with earth is built in which the ceremony is carried on. All the ceremonies seem to be alike in certain particulars such as the use of a sweatbath, the making of many sand paintings, and the singing of a great number of songs. At some point in the ceremony, masked men enter in a procession representing the more important gods of the Navajo. Prayer offerings are made of sections of reeds filled with tobacco, feathers, and pollen. They are painted with the colors and are deposited in the particular situations prescribed for the deity for which they are prepared.

On the last night is held a public performance which is largely attended. In addition to the masked dancers representing the gods, clowns appear who play tricks on each other and often act in a very grotesque manner. The songs and prayers are beautiful in their imagery and have many references to natural elements to which sex is attributed. Varying positions and movements are indicated in an established order. The number four prevails in the prayers and songs themselves, and they are generally repeated four times with minor variations. The following prayer recorded by Doctor Matthews belongs to the Navajo Night Chant.

Tsegihi.
House made of the dawn,
House made of evening light,
House made of the dark cloud,
House made of male rain,
House made of dark mist,
House made of female rain,
House made of pollen,
House made of grasshoppers.
Dark cloud is at the door.
The trail of it is dark cloud.
The zigzag lightning stands high up on it.

Male deity!
Your offering I make,
I have prepared a smoke for you.
Restore my feet for me.
Restore my legs for me.
Restore my body for me.
Restore my mind for me.
Restore my voice for me.
Happily may I walk.
Happily with abundant dark clouds, may I walk.
Happily with abundant showers, may I walk.
Happily with abundant plants, may I walk.
Happily may I walk.

Being as it used to be long ago, may I walk.
May it be happy (or beautiful) before me.
May it be beautiful behind me.

May it be beautiful below me.
May it be beautiful above me.
May it be beautiful all around me.
In beauty it is finished.
In beauty it is finished.

*Beliefs.* While the ceremonies of the Athapascan tribes of the Southwest present considerable specialization and variety, the deities reverenced and the myths related about them are in the main identical. The sun is probably credited with the greatest power and is most frequently referred to in song and addressed in prayer. Among the Jicarilla, at least, the earth is also an object of worship. The Mescalero songs give the moon a place second only to that of the sun. With them the winds are objects of worship as they are also with the Western Apache and the Navajo. The thunder is everywhere feared and looked upon as a mighty power seldom to be mentioned. Clouds and rain, however, have a place of much less importance than with the village people. There are sacred mountains and rivers but these are of necessity different for the different tribes.

One of the more personal gods, Esdzanadlehi, was the sole survivor of a flood or, according to some, the ravages of monsters. She is probably to be identified with the Hopi goddess of hard substances. Naiyenezgani, the culture hero, her grandson, destroyed the monsters and made the world safe for human habitation. By some he is said to have a brother who is, however, among the Apache quite secondary in importance. The Navajo have a series of gods who intervene in human affairs from time to time. They are believed to dwell in the ruins of Canyon de Chelly and in remote places. They are represented in the dances by masked and painted men and receive offerings and are frequently invoked. There are also gods of the water courses and streams. The Jicarilla and the Western Apache know similar gods, in several cases even using the same personal names for them. The Apache more generally use for these gods a generic name, Gan, and individualize them by the use of a color adjective, such as Black Gan. They are analogous to the kachinas of the Pueblo peoples.

The dead are supposed to go to the lower world through the opening by means of which the people originally emerged.

The Indians of the Southwest have many myths and tales, which they relate particularly during the winter. Very many of these myths explain the origin of the world. While these vary in details, according to the tribe and the individual who tells them, they agree as to the general facts. The Athapascan-speaking people tell of a time before the world existed when Spider, Mirage, Whirlwind, and Black Obsidian lived suspended in space. Obsidian rubbed his side and from the removed cuticle produced the earth. They then lifted up the sky and supported it at each of the four corners with a core of obsidian inside a whirlwind. People and animals came to exist within the world in an unexplained manner. They were threatened with a flood and escaped by means of reeds or a ladder through an opening in the sky of the lower world, the crust of this. They were all destroyed by monsters except a girl, Esdzanadlehi. The water pitying her lonely condition became the father of a daughter who in turn by the rays of the rising sun became the mother of Naiyenezgani. This boy visited the sun, his father, withstood severe tests as to his sonship, and secured weapons and the promise of aid. With these weapons he killed a giant, a monster elk or antelope, a great eagle, and many other evil things. When this work was completed and the world was repeopled by the creation of men and women from ears of corn, Esdzanadlehi went to the western ocean, where she is now living in a floating palace of shell. According to the Navajo, Naiyenezgani lives with his brother near the mouth of the San Juan River.

Later, a man who was considered worthless because he gambled away all his property, went down a river in a hollow log, conducted by the gods. He landed at a favorable place and prepared a form for which his pet turkey furnished the seed. He found his way to the home of a man who had all game animals domesticated. He married this man's daughter who received these animals as her marriage portion. Thus was food supplied for mankind.

According to the myths, the various ceremonies of the Navajo were taught to some Indian who by accident or at the direction of the gods went to a ruin or other dwelling place of the supernatural beings and learned there the songs, prayers, and rites.

A long myth explains the origin of the Navajo people and their clans. The nucleus was created by Esdzanadlehi in her western home. As they journeyed westward they met various parties who joined them and who were given names according to the attendant circumstances of their meeting. Other myths explain the origin of fire, and of night and day. There are many animal tales, a large number of them being associated with coyote who is now represented as being exceedingly keen of wit and again as very stupid. These myths and stories told to considerable companies during the evenings of winter are sources both of amusement and instruction.

# CHAPTER V

## CONCLUSION

THE civilization existing in the Southwest, described in the preceding pages, has resulted in part from slow internal growth and in part from borrowings and suggestions received from neighboring cultures. The earliest archaeological evidence shows us a people called Basket Makers, who knew nothing of agriculture, used the spear thrower instead of the bow, and lived a primitive, nomadic life. Later, they did use the bow and began the cultivation of maize. It is now evident that Basket Maker cultures were widespread in southwestern United States and therefore represent the probable background of late Pueblo cultures. Yet, it is still an open question whether the full sequence of cultures from Basket Maker through Pueblo, as now formulated (pp. 27–29), applies to other parts of the Southwest than the San Juan area; but the indications are that it will apply in so far that more primitive Basket Maker cultures preceded pueblo building cultures. In other words, the cliff house and the great ruins like Bonito, Aztec, etc., as well as the modern living Pueblo, stand as an outgrowth of Basket Maker cultures, probably covering the greater part of California and northern Mexico, as well as the States of Utah, Nevada, Colorado, Arizona, and New Mexico.

Whatever may have been the origin of this primitive Basket Maker culture, the culture traits they gradually acquired, as walled houses, maize, beans, cotton, pottery, etc., were not at that time known to their northern and eastern neighbors, but must have been well developed in Mexico and beyond. We are therefore constrained to assume that such important traits as agriculture, pottery, weaving on a loom, the wearing of

sandals, and probably many phases of ceremonial and
religious life came to them from the south.  The order
in which many of these traits reached the San Juan
area has been stated (p. 28).

While such influences did reach the Basket Makers,
it is clear that they developed on original lines.  Thus,
some authorities assume that the architecture of the
Southwest, the honeycomb-like community houses,
often terraced, developed in the Southwest with little

Petroglyphs.  San Juan Valley
(Courtesy of Dr. Prudden)

or no outside stimulus.  The decoration of the pottery
is also a native growth.  It is possible to trace its
development from unfired ware followed by a beginning
of crude black designs on a white background to the
highly ornamented and locally differentiated decorations of the beginning of the Spanish period.  Much of
the elaborate social, political, and ceremonial organization of the present must have developed with the con-
centration of the population into large community
houses.

The pueblo-dwelling peoples of the Rio Grande region have been subjected to constant influence from the tribes of the Plains. They not only received many articles used for food and clothing by trade with these Plains tribes, but periodically became nomads and hunted the buffalo. On the other hand, they themselves seem to have laid the foundation to the basketry art so widespread in western United States and culminating in California.

The Pima and the Papago may represent a southern variety of the culture which existed in the Southwest before the development of elaborate architecture and highly specialized and decorated pottery. It may be, however, that the Pima in particular built great houses and developed a wonderful irrigation system on the Salt River and then, for some reason, reverted to the use of individual family houses. With less plausibility, the same conjectures may be made for the Athapascan-speaking people. It seems more probable in their case that they came into the Southwest from the east, but that their invasion was not very recent.

There still remain many unanswered questions concerning this most interesting region. Some of these will undoubtedly be answered when the studies of the archaeologists have covered the whole region and have pushed further back into the past. It is hoped that detailed statistical studies of the living people and of the abundant skeletal remains may tell at least part of the story of the movements and mingling of the tribes in the past.

# BIBLIOGRAPHY

BANDELIER, A. F.
1881. Historical Introduction to Studies among the Sedentary Indians of New Mexico. Report on the Ruins of the Pueblo of Pecos (Papers, Archaeological Institute of America, American Series no. 1, Boston, 1881).
1890. Final Report of Investigations among the Indians of the Southwestern United States, part I (Papers, Archaeological Institute of America, American Series, no 3, Cambridge, 1890).
1890. Contributions to the History of the Southwestern Portion of the United States (Papers, Archaeological Institute of America, American Series, no. 5, Cambridge, 1890).
1890. The Delight Makers. New York, 1890.
1892. Final Report of Investigations among the Indians of the Southwestern United States, Part II (Papers, Archaeological Institute of America, American Series, no 4, Cambridge, 1892).

BOLTON, H. E.
1916. Spanish Exploration of the Southwest, 1542–1706. New York, 1916.

BOURKE, JOHN G.
1884. The Snake-Dance of the Moquis of Arizona. New York, 1884.

BUNZEL, RUTH L.
✓ 1929. The Pueblo Potter. New York, 1929.

CUSHING, F. H.
1883. Zuñi Fetiches (Second Annual Report, Bureau of Ethnology, Washington, 1883).
1896. Outlines of Zuñi Creation Myths (Thirteenth Annual Report, Bureau of American Ethnology, Washington, 1896).
1901. Zuñi Folk-tales. New York, 1901.
1920. Zuñi Breadstuff (Indian Notes and Monographs, Museum of the American Indian, Heye Foundation, vol. 8, New York, 1920).

DORSEY, G. A. AND VOTH, H. R.
1901. The Oraibi Soyal Ceremony (Publication 55, Field Columbian Museum, Anthropological Series, vol. 3, no. 1, Chicago, 1901).

1902. The Mishongnovi Ceremonies of the Snake and Antelope Fraternities (Publication 66, Field Columbian Museum Anthropological Series, vol. 3, no. 3, Chicago, 1902).

DOUGLASS, A. E.
1929. Secret of the Southwest solved by Talkative Tree Rings (The National Geographic Magazine, vol. 56, pp. 737–770, Washington, 1929).

DUMAREST, N.
1919. Notes on Cochiti, New Mexico (Memoirs, American Anthropological Association, vol. 6, no. 3, 1919).

FEWKES, J. W.
1898. Archaeological Expedition to Arizona in 1895 (Seventeenth Annual Report, Bureau of American Ethnology, part 2, Washington, 1898).

1900. Tusayan Migration Traditions (Nineteenth Annual Report, Bureau of American Ethnology, part 2, Washington, 1900).

1904. Two Summers' Work in Pueblo Ruins (Twenty-second Annual Report, Bureau of American Ethnology, part 1, Washington, 1904).

1907. Excavations at Casa Grande, Arizona, in 1906–1907 (Smithsonian Miscellaneous Collections, vol. 50, pp. 289–329, Washington, 1907).

1909. Antiquities of the Mesa Verde National Park; Spruce-Tree House (Bulletin 41, Bureau of American Ethnology, Washington, 1909).

1911. Antiquities of the Mesa Verde National Park; Cliff Palace (Bulletin 51, Bureau of American Ethnology, Washington, 1911).

1912. Casa Grande, Arizona (Twenty-eighth Annual Report, Bureau of American Ethnology, Washington, 1912).

FRANCISCAN FATHERS
1910. An Ethnologic Dictionary of the Navaho Language. St. Michaels, Arizona, 1910.

FREIRE-MARRECO, B.
1914. Tewa Kinship Terms from the Pueblo of Hano, Arizona (American Anthropologist, n.s. vol. 16, pp. 269–287, 1914).

GODDARD, P. E.
1911. Jicarilla Apache Texts (Anthropological Papers, American Museum of Natural History, vol. 8, New York, 1911).

1918. Myths and Tales of the San Carlos Apache (Anthropological Papers, American Museum of Natural History, vol. 24, part 1, New York, 1918).

1919. Myths and Tales of the White Mountain Apache (Anthropological Papers, American Mueum of Natural History, vol. 24, part 2, New York, 1919).

GOLDFRANK, ESTHER SCHIFF

1927. The Social and Ceremonial Organization of Cochiti (Memoirs, American Anthropological Association, no. 33, 1927).

GUERNSEY, S. J. AND KIDDER, A. V.

1921. Basket-Maker Caves of Northeastern Arizona (Papers, Peabody Museum of American Archaeology and Ethnology, vol. 8, no. 2, Cambridge, 1921).

GUTHE, CARL E.

1925. Pueblo Pottery Making. New Haven, 1925.

HAEBERLIN, H. K.

1916. The Idea of Fertilization in the Culture of the Pueblo Indians (Memoirs, American Anthropological Association, vol. 3, no. 1, 1916).

HARRINGTON, J. P.

1916. The Ethnogeography of the Tewa Indians (Twenty-ninth Annual Report, Bureau of American Ethnology, Washington, 1916).

HEWETT, EDGAR L.

1906. Antiquities of the Jemez Plateau, New Mexico (Bulletin 32, Bureau of American Ethnology, Washington, 1906).

HODGE, F. W.

1893. Prehistoric Irrigation in Arizona (American Anthropologist, o.s. vol. 6, pp. 323–330, Washington, 1893).

1896. Pueblo Indian Clans (American Anthropologist, o.s. vol. 9, pp. 472–498, Washington, 1896).

1920. Hawikuh Bonework (Indian Notes and Monographs, Museum of the American Indian, Heye Foundation, vol. 3, no. 3, New York, 1920).

1921. Turquoise Work of Hawikuh, New Mexico (Leaflets, Museum of the American Indian, Heye Foundation, no. 2, New York, 1921).

HOLMES, W. H.

1878. Report of the Ancient Ruins of Southwestern Colorado, examined during the summers of 1875 and 1876 (Tenth Annual Report, United States Geological and Geographical Survey of the Territories, 1876, Washington, 1878).

1886.   Pottery of the Ancient Pueblos (Fourth Annual Report, Bureau of Ethnology, Washington, 1886).

HOUGH, W.
1907.   Antiquities of the Upper Gila and Salt River Valleys in Arizona and New Mexico (Bulletin 35, Bureau of American Ethnology, Washington, 1907.

1914.   Culture of the Ancient Pueblos of the Upper Gila River Region, New Mexico and Arizona (Bulletin 87, United States National Museum, Washington, 1914).

✓ 1915.   The Hopi Indians. Cedar Rapids, Iowa, 1915.

JACKSON, W. H.
1878.   Report on the Ancient Ruins examined in 1875 and 1876 (Annual Report, United States Geological and Geographical Survey of the Territories, 1876, Washington, 1878).

JEANÇON, J. A.
1923.   Excavations in the Chama Valley, New Mexico (Bulletin 81, Bureau of American Ethnology, Washington, 1923).

KIDDER, A. V.
1915.   Pottery of the Pajarito Plateau and of some Adjacent Regions in New Mexico (Memoirs, American Anthropological Association, vol. 2, part 6, Lancaster, 1915).

1916.   The Pottery of the Casas Grandes District, Chihuahua (Holmes Anniversary Volume, Washington, 1916).

✓ 1924.   An Introduction to the Study of Southwestern Archaeology. New Haven, 1924.

KIDDER, A. V. AND GUERNSEY, S. J.
1919.   Archaeological Explorations in Northeastern Arizona (Bulletin 65, Bureau of American Ethnology, Washington, 1919).

KISSELL, MARY LOIS
1916.   Basketry of the Papago and Pima (Anthropological Papers, American Museum of Natural History, vol. 17, part 4, New York, 1916).

KROEBER, A. L.
1902.   Preliminary Sketch of the Mohave Indians (American Anthropologist, n.s. vol. 4, pp. 276–285, 1902).

1917.   Zuñi Kin and Clan (Anthropological Papers, American Museum of Natural History, vol. 18, part 2, New York, 1917).

LLOYD, J. WM.
   1911. Awawtam, Indian Nights, being the Myths and Legends of the Pimas of Arizona, Westfield, N. J., 1911.
LUMHOLTZ, CARL
   1911. New Trails in Mexico. New York, 1912.
LUMMIS, C. F.
   1893. The Land of Poco Tiempo. New York, 1893.
   1894. The Man who married the Moon and other Pueblo Indian Folk-Stories, New York, 1894.
MASON, J. ALDEN
   1920. The Papago Harvest Festival (American Anthropologist, n.s. vol. 22, pp. 13-25, 1920).
MATTHEWS, WASHINGTON
   1887. The Mountain Chant (Fifth Annual Report, Bureau of American Ethnology, Washington, 1887).
   1897. Navaho Legends (Memoirs, American Folk-Lore Society, vol. 5, 1897; reprinted, New York, 1925).
   1902. The Night Chant (Memoirs, American Museum of Natural History, vol. 6, New York, 1902).
MINDELEFF, COSMOS
   1896. Casa Grande Ruin (Thirteenth Annual Report, Bureau of American Ethnology, Washington, 1896).
   1897. Cliff Ruins of the Cañon de Chelly, Arizona (Sixteenth Annual Report, Bureau of American Ethnology, Washington, 1897).
   1898. Navaho Houses (Seventeenth Annual Report, Bureau of American Ethnology, part 2, Washington, 1898).
   1900. Localization of Tusayan Clans (Nineteenth Annual Report, Bureau of American Ethnology, Washington, 1900).
MINDELEFF, VICTOR
   1891. A Study in Pueblo Architecture: Tusayan and Cibola (Eighth Annual Report, Bureau of American Ethnology, Washington, 1891).
MORRIS, EARL H.
   1919. Preliminary Account of the Antiquities of the Region between the Mancos and La Plata Rivers in Southwestern Colorado (Thirty-third Annual Report, Bureau of American Ethnology, Washington, 1919)
   1919. The Aztec Ruin (Anthropological Papers, American Museum of Natural History, vol. 26, part 1, New York, 1919).

1921.    The House of the Great Kiva at the Aztec Ruin (Anthropological Papers, American Museum of Natural History, vol. 26, part 2, New York, 1921).

1927.    The Beginnings of Pottery Making in the San Juan Area; Unfired Prototypes and the Wares of the Earliest Ceramic Period (Anthropological Papers, American Museum of Natural History, vol. 28, part 2, New York, 1927).

1928.    Notes on Excavations in the Aztec Ruin (Anthropological Papers, American Museum of Natural History, vol. 26, part 5, New York, 1928).

NELSON, N. C.

1914.    Pueblo Ruins of the Galisteo Valley (Anthropological. Papers, American Museum of Natural History, vol. 15, part 1, New York, 1914).

NORDENSKIÖLD, G.

1893.    The Cliff Dwellers of the Mesa Verde, Southwestern Colorado, Their Pottery and Implements. Translated by D. Lloyd Morgan. Stockholm, 1893.

PARSONS, ELSIE CLEWS

1917.    Notes on Zuñi (Memoirs, American Anthropological Association, vol. 4, nos. 3–4, 1917).

1918.    Notes on Acoma and Laguna (American Anthropologist, n.s. vol. 20, pp. 162–186, 1918).

1920.    Notes on Ceremonialism at Laguna (Anthropological Papers, American Museum of Natural History, vol. 19, part 4, New York, 1920).

1923.    Laguna Genealogies (Anthropological Papers, American Museum of Natural History, vol. 19, part 5, New York, 1923).

1927.    A Pueblo Indian Journal (Memoirs, American Anthropological Association, no. 32, 1927).

PEPPER, G. H.

1920.    Pueblo Bonito (Anthropological Papers, American Museum of Natural History, vol. 27, New York, 1920).

PRUDDEN, T. MITCHELL

1914.    The Circular Kivas of Small House Ruins in the San Juan Watershed (American Anthropologist, n.s. vol. 16, pp. 33–58, Lancaster, 1914).

1918.    A Further Study of Prehistoric Small House Ruins in the San Juan Watershed (Memoirs, American Anthropological Association, vol. 5, no. 1, Lancaster, 1918).

Russell, F.
    1908.  The Pima Indians (Twenty-sixth Annual Report, Bureau of
          American Ethnology, Washington, 1908).

Spier, Leslie
    1917.  An Outline for a Chronology of Zuñi Ruins (Anthropological
          Papers, American Museum of Natural History, vol.
          18, part 2, New York, 1917).
    1918.  Notes on Some Little Colorado Ruins (Anthropological
          Papers, American Museum of Natural History, vol.
          18, part 4, New York, 1918).
    1919.  Ruins in the White Mountains, Arizona (Anthropological
          Papers, American Museum of Natural History, vol. 18,
          part 5, New York, 1919).
    1928.  Havasupai Ethnography (Anthropological Papers, Am-
          erican Museum of Natural History, vol 29, part 3,
          New York, 1928).

Starr, F.
    1899.  Census of Cochiti (Proceedings, Davenport Academy of
          Sciences, vol. 7, pp. 33–45, 1899).

Stevenson, M. C.
    1894.  The Sia (Eleventh Annual Report, Bureau of American
          Ethnology, Washington, 1894).
    1904.  The Zuñi Indians (Twenty-third Annual Report, Bureau of
          American Ethnology, Washington, 1904).

Twitchell, R. E.
    1911.  The Leading Facts of New Mexican History. Cedar Rapids,
          Iowa, 1911.
    1914.  The Spanish Archives of New Mexico. Cedar Rapids,
          Iowa, 1914.

Voth, H. R.
    1901.  The Oraibi Powamu Ceremony (Publication 61, Field
          Columbian Museum, Anthropological Series, vol. 3,
          no. 3, Chicago, 1901).
    1903.  The Oraibi Summer Snake Ceremony (Publication 83,
          Field Columbian Museum, Anthropological Series,
          vol. 3, no. 4, Chicago, 1903).
    1903.  The Oraibi Oaqol Ceremony (Publication 84, Field Colum-
          bian Museum, Anthropological Series, vol. 6, no. 1,
          Chicago, 1903).
    1906.  Oraibi Natal Customs and Ceremonies (Publication 97,
          Field Columbian Museum, Anthropological Series,
          vol. 6, no. 2, Chicago, 1905).

Winship, G. P.
　　1896.　The Coronado Expedition, 1540–1542 (Fourteenth Annual
　　　　Report, Bureau of American Ethnology, part 1,
　　　　Washington, 1896).